"*Do we or do we not believe in government of the people? The citizens of America are ready for a leadership that will speak to them directly. They're fed up with inflation and with big government, and they sense that there's a definite relationship between the two. . . .*"

—Ronald Reagan

Ronald Reagan's Call to Action

presents in his own words exactly where Reagan stands on the major issues that confront Americans today—welfare, fiscal responsibility, the problems of the cities, national defense, the greatness of America and the problems of the future.

It is a clear statement of the ideas that drive him and an illustration of how he has carried them out in actual practice.

It is a book to examine and ponder in this critical election year—1976.

RONALD REAGAN'S
CALL TO ACTION

**Ronald Reagan
with Charles D. Hobbs**

WARNER BOOKS

A Warner Communications Company

WARNER BOOKS EDITION
First Printing: March, 1976

Library of Congress Catalog Card Number: 75-45220

"How Ronald Reagan Governed California" by Charles Hobbs
originally appeared in the *National Review* January 17, 1975,
pages 147-173. Reprinted by permission.

This Warner Books Edition is published by
arrangement with Thomas Nelson, Inc.

Cover design by Gene Light

Cover photograph by Bill Ray © TIME-LIFE Picture Agency

Warner Books, Inc., 75 Rockefeller Plaza, New York, N.Y. 10019

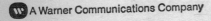 A Warner Communications Company

Printed in the United States of America

Not associated with Warner Press, Inc. of Anderson, Indiana

To our future:
Ronald Reagan

Contents

Foreword

This book presents Ronald Reagan's political philosophy as he presented it to me in a series of taped interviews in the spring and early summer of 1975. The interviews were informal: just the two of us discussing his views on the nation and its problems. A few days in advance of each interview I would let him know what subjects I wanted to cover, but I don't think he spent much time preparing himself on those subjects. He didn't need any special preparation: he had already thought through his positions on the issues, and he stayed up to date by what must have been a prodigious reading of current books, newspapers, and magazines. Also, it was a time when he had many other things to do.

He had left the governorship of California three months earlier, not seeking reelection, and thus carrying out the belief he had stated in the 1966 campaign that no one should serve more than two terms as California's governor. The national recession hit during his last few months as governor and, as soon as he left office, he began to accept invitations on the "mashed potato circuit," speaking to groups of every size and political persuasion across the country. His theme, one that will be found throughout this book, was that government is the problem, not the solution, in combating recession, inflation, unemployment, and the other ills plaguing the nation. He had many times more invitations than he could accept, even though he was giving three or four speeches a week. He was also doing a weekly syndicated newspaper column and a five-times-a-week network radio commentary. In between he found time to talk with me and my tape recorder.

My problem was trying to keep up with his schedule. One of our conversations was held on a commercial airliner between Los Angeles and Washington, D.C., and the tape included a running commentary by the pilot on the scenic beauties of an America which was, as I remember it, mostly cloudy and dark as we flew over it.

And cloudy and dark in more ways than one. We were then nearing the bottom of what was turning out to be the worst recession since the thirties, and I was skeptical that we could pull out of it without a full-scale depression. Reagan shared my concern, but not my pessimism. And as we talked I found, somewhat to my chagrin, that my own faith in the nation was being renewed by Reagan's optimism. Although I had known him as the "citizen-politician" who was governor of California, I had never had the opportunity to explore in any depth his personal beliefs. I found that his personal and political philosophies are identical, and that he is the same in private as he is in public: the same person as a private citizen as he was as a public official. He is honest, says what he believes, and does what he says he will do—all in all, a unique individual in the world of professional politics.

The more we talked, the more I came to understand that "citizen-politician" means to Reagan first of all a citizen who trusts the judgment of his fellow citizens and is dedicated to improving their opportunities for individual choice, and second a practical politician who can work out legitimate and effective ways to make those improvements happen.

As you will find, if I have done justice to his ideas, Reagan's political philosophy is strong, clear, and simple: strong, but not arbitrary; clear, but not dogmatic; and simple, but not simplistic. These distinctions must be made because Reagan, like other outspoken leaders, has suffered at the hands of a working press that, for varying reasons and in varying degrees, tends to portray strength as arbitrary, dogmatic, and simplistic. And there certainly are politicians who find their ideas so appealing and so "right" that they only talk and never listen.

Not so Reagan. During the interviews his obvious interest in hearing my opinions resulted in embarrassingly long segments of my own voice on the tapes. Yet I never doubted where he stood on any issue, and he was not afraid to let me know when he could not completely resolve an issue in his own mind because there was, as he put it, "so much right on both sides."

But, on issue after issue, Reagan demonstrated a consistent faith and confidence in the ability of an informed electorate to make the right choices. Certainly as we talked, institutions came under fire, programs were criticized, individuals were faulted for bad judgment. Nothing, however, moved Reagan from the belief that the American people could, with honest, forthright, and intelligent leadership, overcome any problem they might have to face.

To produce a faithful distillation of our conversations, I have focused on the issues that concern all of the people, not just those with an ax to grind or a cause to celebrate. This approach was dictated by Reagan's beliefs. He is today's most articulate and consistent spokesman for the idea that individual liberty is the key to national strength and survival. His unbounded faith in the people and the nation is grounded in the freedom of every individual to decide his own fate, with the least possible interference from bureaucrats or autocrats, public or private.

It is my hope that this book will remove for some of its readers the labels that have been pasted on Reagan's image by both his friends and his foes. I found him, as I think you will, to be a man without cynicism or guile, a man who believes in himself and his country, a man who hopes for and expects to find the same self-confidence and national pride in others, and a man who tells you what he believes, clearly and candidly.

To all those who cherish liberty and value law

Part I

The Philosophy

The Individual

Ronald Reagan's philosophy is founded on the sacredness of the individual. Understanding that about Reagan is essential to understanding anything else he believes in. His first belief is in the inviolability of the rights of you, and me, and himself, and every other human being to do as he or she wishes short of infringing on the rights of others to do the same.

Reagan's personal concern for and commitment to individual liberty are an article of faith, because for him liberty is the cornerstone of democracy in America. Liberty means individual, everyday freedoms:

. . . the basic freedoms: the freedom to worship, the freedom to choose your occupation, the freedom to try and to fail and, if need be, to try again, the freedom to make mistakes and to do things others might consider stupid.

We were discussing Reagan's concept of liberty in his office overlooking an enormous parking lot behind a federal office building in Los Angeles. A day earlier 4,000 motorcyclists had paraded through the city to that parking lot, where they met to protest proposals for federal regulations to require all motorcycle riders to wear helmets. Reagan sympathized with the cyclists.

You know, I would support anything that would make the motorcycle safer where others besides the riders might be endangered. And I happen to

think a rider's stupid if he doesn't wear all the protective devices available. But, if he chooses not to, it's none of government's business.

Democracy based on the belief in individual liberty must be carefully protected—not because it is fragile, but because it is so rare. There are always those ready to appropriate the word "democracy" to their own uses, uses that invariably include the bending of our liberties to their wills.

I think one of the most dangerous slogans ever coined is "the greatest good for the greatest number." A noble-sounding phrase, but what does it really mean? It means that 50% of the people plus one can do whatever they want to the rest, by rationalizing that what they're doing to them is "good." The greatness of our country has been and must continue to be that you can stand alone against all of the other 211 million people. You have certain basic rights which they cannot take away from you, even by unanimous vote.

Yet in discussing the specific problems of our society, discussions that make up the rest of this book, it is clear that our basic rights are being eroded, even though the people have not voted them away. Of five aspects of American life that Reagan considers intimately related to our ability to remain free—family unity, individual morality, material well-being, enlightenment through education, and equality of opportunity—only in the last of these does he think that there has been significant progress in the past few decades. And even that progress has been unnecessarily slowed by the clumsy mistakes of government, primarily at the federal level.

Everybody's entitled to an equal start and must be allowed to advance as far and as fast as his own ability takes him. But many of the government programs have actually violated the principles of freedom and reward for effort that give meaning to equal opportunity. I remember one—in the Great Society days—in which the purpose was to find after-school jobs for delinquent kids who were dropping out of school in New York, on the theory that the reason they were dropping out and getting in trouble was lack of money. So they hired the delinquents and laid off good kids who were doing the same jobs. What happened? It didn't take a kid 15 minutes to figure out that if being good didn't pay off, being bad did: that the thing to do if you needed a job was to break a window with a brick and stand around until you were caught. That form of equal opportunity is insanity. But overall, despite the mistakes of well-intentioned but uninformed social planners, and despite the purposeful distortions of those dedicated to changing our whole form of government, I think there is now a more general recognition that everyone is entitled to that equal start in life.

Equal opportunity is a hollow victory for our society, however, if all of the opportunities become constantly smaller and smaller. If inflation continues to erode our standard of living, if the products of our schools are less educated, if the breakup of families and breakdown of moral values produce more unhappy and insecure people: are we not simply equalizing the opportunity to fail? And with what result?

The result is that we're beginning to ignore the essential difference of this country, which is the sacredness of the individual. If we keep going in that direction, there can be one outcome: our surrender to a totally government-planned and government-controlled society. There are people pushing hard for this to happen. And when it happens it will be called the "fulfillment of the liberal dream." But in fact it will be fascism, because that's what fascism is: private ownership with total government control. Before that moment comes we have to make the people aware of the danger . . . and we don't have much time left.

Most people seem to pursue personal security at least as avidly as they do personal independence. **"There's no such thing as real security from the day you're born, and yet, all of us want to feel the security that doesn't really exist."** Desire for security has encouraged, and now in turn is being fed by **". . . big government, big business, big labor."** But only the people can protect and be secure in their own liberty.

If the people find out that most of their insecurity is created by the very effort through government to provide security, I believe they still have the strength to reestablish their personal independence, and to gain with it a measure of security they have never known before. But they must be told the facts about how government controls their lives and their choices. The opportunity is there because right now they are leery of big government, big business, and big labor. But mostly they fear big government, and rightly so.

The first responsibility of every citizen, then, is **". . . to join with his fellow citizens to preserve the ultimate in individual freedom consistent with an orderly society."**

Equal opportunity, advancement based on ability, the right to be independent and to succeed or fail on one's own judgment, the sacredness of the individual and the inviolability of his rights, and the responsibility to preserve individual freedom and respect for the rights of all: these are at the heart of Ronald Reagan's concept of realistic democracy.

The Family

A child in America should grow up with the assurance that his parents have accepted the responsibility for defining right and wrong.

The transmission of values from one generation to the next is as vital to spiritual progress as the transmission of knowledge is to material progress. In our society, as in every other enlightened society in history, the family has been the essential institution for the transmission of traditional and stabilizing values. Dictators have almost always tried to destroy the family.

If you look at the dictatorial systems, the totalitarian systems, you'll notice that one of the first things they do is take over the teaching of the child at an early age, so that the government can instruct him on what is right and wrong. Russia has systematically removed the children from their parents. Hitler did the same thing with his youth movement. Children were actually taught to spy on their parents.

The most stable civilizations have all been based on strong family ties. But government, even a socalled benevolent government, can break those ties irrevocably. Years ago, when the Philippine Islands were a territory of the United States, we decided to extend Social Security benefits to the Philippine people. Up to that time families had been extremely close—three generations living together

23

in the home. But Social Security, by removing the dependence of family members on each other, destroyed the whole family bond. And with it, as we learned later, we effectively destroyed their society. How often that's been the outcome of social reform!

Many people in our society are confused about how a family should function, and particularly about the relationships between parents and children. Psychiatrists, psychologists, sociologists, and other students of man and society offer a myriad of prescriptions for improved family functioning. Artificial props to family unity are offered; parent-child relationships are explored and explained. Just what are the duties of a parent? And of a child?

I don't think it's necessary to win a popularity contest with your kids, and especially not while they're kids. Parents should be more concerned with what their kids will think of them when they reach thirty. Or, more importantly, what their kids will think of themselves. Most of us, when we look back over our own lives and our reactions to our parents, discover that today we accept and are grateful for things we rebelled against at the age of fifteen or twenty.

But as parents we often act as if we were afraid to be parents. Something has made us overly desirous of pleasing our children. I don't know if it was the feeling of being deprived in the generation that grew up in the Depression, and I don't think the experts have begun to solve that problem. But I do know that we've swallowed what I'd call the "Dr. Spock syndrome," wherein we question our own values and whether we have a right to impose our beliefs on our children. And in doing so, we've weakened the family. A child in America should grow up with the assurance that his parents have accepted the responsibility for defining right and wrong.

24

Can schools and churches substitute for the family as purveyors of moral values?

They can for a few individuals, but not for the society. Both schools and churches are necessary for support, but they can never be a total substitute. There is a growing tendency for schools and even some churches to challenge the mores and values of parents, to encourage a young person to develop his own ideas and standards. That's healthy only if the young person already has the maturity of having accepted and lived with a set of values in his own family. Otherwise he is likely to fall victim to the first doctrinaire teacher or minister who gets to him, just to maintain a sense of security. That's when education becomes indoctrination.

One of the most noticeable changes in family life has been the trend toward isolation. The family, much smaller and less varied in age and experience than it used to be, has become more a place to hide from the world than a place to face it. Reagan came from a family that faced the world.

I was raised in a small town atmosphere, and I can remember going for walks on summer evenings with my father and mother. We'd start down the street, just strolling, in that wonderful summer twilight. And we'd pass houses—everybody had a front porch, unlike the back patios of today that you can't see from the street—and as we passed we'd wave and maybe stop and call up to somebody on the porch. And they'd say, "Come on up and sit for a while." We kids would sit on the steps and the grownups would sit on the porch swing and chairs. Mainly—you know how kids love to overhear adults' conversations—we would listen, just listen to our parents and neighbors talk about what was going on and what they thought of it. And the stars would come out, and then we'd get up and go home. That was a kind of "social security" that no government could provide. Now, unfortunately, most of us live in places where we don't even know our neighbors.

One of the more important functions of a family is to be a seedbed for other families. In order to fulfill this function, parents must be willing to let their children grow up.

I don't feel that a family should cling to its young to the point that they're reluctant to leave the nest. Quite the contrary. I think the whole duty of parents is to bring their children up with a sense of values to the point where, with confidence, they can throw them out of the nest and start them on their way.

There can be little doubt that the family has deteriorated as a force in American life. And with that deterioration have come an uncertainty about moral standards and a tendency for individuals to define their own morality without regard for people close to them.

When kids get into a debate with their parents about whether someone has done something morally right or wrong and they try to resolve the problem by asking, "Well, by whose standards?" then you begin to realize why this wave of hedonism we're experiencing is able to grow and spread.

"If it feels good, do it." "Whatever's right." But right for whom? "If it feels good, do it" is a good slogan until someone wants to feel good by hitting you over the head.

There are hopeful signs, however, for the renaissance of the family as a morally persuasive institution.

The Mormon Church, for example, is making a concerted effort to restore the family. They didn't wait for the government to develop a program for

26

family unity. They just suddenly declared that Monday night is family night. There are no church services or functions planned for that night, and the Church urges families to stay home and have family discussions. And each family is provided with a book of suggested things to do, topics to discuss. The family has the kind of discussion that probably took place much more often before radio and television were invented. I understand that the Mormon idea is so successful that most of the people—even the young people—have come to regard this not as a church chore, but as a time of great enjoyment and interest.

If every family would dedicate itself, starting tomorrow, simply to sustaining itself as a family unit, and if all parents would dedicate themselves to communicating their beliefs and moral values to their children, the wave of hedonism would end abruptly. I don't mean that all families would stay together simply by trying, or that all kids would grow up to be models of virtue. But throughout our society standards for acceptable behavior based on family ties would be reestablished, and we would find we needed a lot less "social reform" and a lot fewer government programs.

An Orderly Society

The words used to describe theoretical political and economic systems are always inadequate to describe real nations. Russian communism is only an approximation, and then only of one phase, of the theoretical communism described by Karl Marx. Historical evidence seems to indicate that Russia has already gone as far as she will go toward the theoretical classless society of Marx. Perhaps a classless society cannot be reached at all; perhaps it cannot be reached through totalitarianism; perhaps it cannot be reached through the dictator-led state socialism that Russia practices in the name of communism. In any event, although "communism" does not describe precisely the political and economic system of Russia, it is the word Russia uses to describe herself and the word that best describes the theoretical underpinnings of the Russian state.

The same lack of precision occurs in describing the United States as a capitalistic democracy. Capitalism is an economic system in which the ways and means of accumulating wealth are in private hands, and in which goods and services are exchanged in a free market. By definition any government regulation that distorts and makes less "free" the free market is anticapitalistic. Democracy is a political system in which the supreme power is vested in the people and exercised by them through free elections. A capitalistic democracy, then, is most simply a free-market nation governed by its citizens through free elections.

The United States is somewhat less than a perfect

democracy, and far less than perfect capitalism. More important than the lack of theoretical purity to Reagan, however, is the steady retreat of the nation from the principles of capitalistic democracy on which it was built.

The trend today is toward more and more control of the economy by government. That goes directly against our traditions, against the ideas of freedom and individual initiative that made us great. For years we increased our productivity faster than all other nations; now we rank fourteenth in rate of productivity increase.

Continued government growth was an invention of Franklin Roosevelt's New Deal. Roosevelt's Secretary of the Treasury, Henry Morgenthau, Jr., gave it impetus by deciding to use taxing power for regulation of behavior. He even said publicly that taxes were intended to both punish and reward behavior that the government wanted to discourage or encourage. Since then it has been incorrect to think of taxes only as the most efficient means of raising the money needed by government. They have become an economic and social tool of government social reformers to control our actions and choices.

And not only taxes. To fund the federal deficit this year, the federal government is borrowing an estimated 80% of the available private capital, cutting off four-fifths of the capital normally available to the private sector to create new jobs and increase production for our growing population. The sad fact is that through the combination of taxation and regulation the government has taken effective control of our economy.

There's no question that the self-sufficiency and material well-being of Americans are being diminished by government. We're following England down the road to intellectual and financial destruction.

The British writer Malcolm Muggeridge pointed out last year that the literacy rate in England is now dropping —probably the last and fatal symptom of the national socialist disease. Muggeridge went on to say wryly that at the present rate of increase in expenditures for education, the entire gross national product would be spent on education at just the time the entire population becomes illiterate.

It used to be said that we lagged behind England in social reform by about 20 years. We're catching up rapidly, and apparently our leaders can't or won't learn the plain object lesson of England's deterioration. They still nod when people tell them that we ought to have a certain program because England has it.

It's tragic to look at England today and compare it to the England that fought the Battle of Britain 35 years ago. To think what they withstood and what they accomplished: the nobility of that entire people. I doubt it could happen today.

But we didn't start this country to imitate Europe. We started this country to get away from the mistakes that had been made in Europe and the rest of the world. We started this country to be free and independent. And we're still the only country that has people from all the other countries in the world waiting to get into it.

Americans still have a great deal of generosity and compassion down deep inside: government hasn't yet regulated it away. That concern for others is what's holding our society together in the face of government's attempts to make numbers of us.

On one of my radio broadcasts last year I told the story of a man and his son traveling to Chicago by plane. The boy was quite ill and was being taken to a Chicago hospital for treatment; the father was an unemployed construction worker. The father lost his wallet on the plane, and the crew and passengers helped him search for it, but to no avail. Before they landed in Chicago, the crew took up a collection, since the father and his son didn't even have enough money to get from the airport to the hospital. The father insisted on taking their names so he could pay them back. After the plane took off again with a new load of passengers, the stewardesses continued the search for the wallet. When the new passengers found out what the problem was, they insisted on taking up another collection throughout the plane. And when the stewardess made the return trip through Chicago, she delivered several hundred dollars to the man and his son, gifts from people who had never seen them but had heard the story and wanted to help.

I think this attitude still prevails among the American people, but if government keeps on . . .

American government has three tiers: federal, state, and local. Defenders of government like to point out that, as a result, "government" is not monolithic, and its effects on people and society should not be credited to a single force. As evidence, these defenders point to the rapid growth of local taxes and diverse local governments.

It's true that in the last 20 years local taxes have grown even faster than federal taxes. But the important thing to remember about that fact is why. It wasn't because the people demanded that their city councils and county boards raise property and sales taxes. It was because the federal government forced local governments to participate in so-called federal sharing programs. Federal pressure reduced the options of local governments and thus the freedom of local citizens to decide what their governments should be doing.

Here's how a sharing program works. The federal government offers a dollar to a state for a specific purpose, contingent upon the state or some local government within it putting up another dollar for the same purpose. The irony is that, while the federal government says it's sharing in the cost of a local program, the exact opposite is the case. It's the state or local government that's forced to share in the cost of a federal program in order to get federal money.

Of course, it's all the same money, yours and mine, but it makes a tremendous difference who decides what to do with it. For example, suppose a city needs a general hospital, and the federal government says it will pay half the costs of a treatment center for the mentally handicapped. What city would have the nerve to say it doesn't need such a center, especially when a few of its potential general hospital patients are mentally handicapped? The outcome, of course, is that the city puts up its half of the treatment center money and also builds a general hospital, slightly smaller and less efficient than originally planned. The city ends up paying 30% to 50% more to meet its real needs, and the local taxpayers foot the bill.

The major federal sharing programs are health, welfare, and highways. They all share the same carrot and stick characteristics; they all start out looking to local officials like sugar-candy carrots and end up being bludgeons over the heads of the local taxpayers.

It's been suggested that the federal government get rid of sharing programs and turn over the same amount of money to state and local governments with no strings attached—in the form of block grants. That's not a bad idea, but it doesn't go far enough. Revenue sharing was supposed to do just that, but the political pressures in Washington turned it into just another sharing program piled on top of the others.

We should not just substitute block grants for sharing programs but should also give the states the opportunity to recapture the tax base for that money. Allow the states, up to the limit of the block grant program, to trigger, through raises in state taxes, a deduction in federal taxes from that state. Then the real decision-making power about how to use the grant money would rest with the states.

How big an effect does the government have on our society? Here are two measures. The revenues that government collects each year currently equal about half of the combined annual earnings of all Americans. What's more, government expenditures are growing at one and a half times the rate of the economy. The second measure is land. Forty percent of the land in the United States is owned by government, and use of the rest is controlled by government regulation, which each year grows more and more stringent and centralized.

Almost a hundred years ago, in 1878, Senator Benjamin Hill said, "I do not dread industrial corporations as instruments of power to destroy this country. But there is one corporation we may all dread: that corporation is the federal government. If this ambitious, ever-growing corporation become oppressive, who shall check it. If it become unjust, who shall trust it. Watch and guard with sleepless dread that corporation which can make all property and the rights of all states and people, all liberty and hope, its playthings in an hour, its victims forever." Senator Hill must have been a very astute man to see that a century ago.

The question is not whether government is the controlling force in our society, but who or what controls government. It certainly is not the collective wills of individual citizens, and seldom is it the expressed will of the majority.

Government, when it is bent at all, is bent to the wills of special interest groups, whose goals are always in opposition to the general interest. Although the special interests represent a minority viewpoint, they are so highly organized to get what they want from government that they override the influence of the general public. The great mass of people has been too busy working to pay the bills and the taxes; they're not organized. They only get a chance to make their will known at election time.

Special interest groups form and work toward a goal with little or no concern for the effects on others. In many cases they join together for more strength. The environmentalists and the consumer advocates are an example. The places where their goals overlap are insignificant compared to the individual gains they expect from teaming up.

The shift of economic and social control to government is one of the two major shifts in our society in this century. The other is the shift of people from the country to the city.

Thomas Jefferson always hoped that America would develop into a predominantly rural nation, and he admitted that the government had been structured to give a little more weight in the vote to what he called the "yeomanry." He thought that people living on the land, with plenty of living space around them, would always be more dedicated than city dwellers to personal liberty and independence.

I was raised in a rural setting, and I've lived most of my adult life in cities, and there's no question to me that most people change when they come to live in a city. They build up a shell that shuts out other people. Maybe it's a defense mechanism because they rub elbows and bump into each other all day long.

I've always been struck by how close together tables are in New York restaurants. From the lowliest hash house to the plushest restaurant, you sit down with your shoulders virtually touching the fellow's shoulders at the next table. And peo-

34

ple don't lower their voices; they go right on discussing their most personal and intimate affairs as if nobody were within 50 feet of them. They're not listening to other people, and they don't expect to be listened to. Being forced to live crowded together, they've developed a protective mechanism to make them think they're not crowded. They simply don't pay any attention to other people.

A few years ago the Candid Camera television program presented a graphic example of what I mean. They set up their hidden cameras on a city street and had a man lie motionless in the gutter. Then they trained their cameras on the passersby to get their reactions. Apparently they anticipated that people would stop, look at the man in the gutter, look at each other, wonder out loud if they should call the police or what they should do. Well, no one stopped. They all looked straight ahead or up at the buildings or at the store windows. Some had to change directions, to skirt around the man's body, but not one human being stopped or even looked down at him. No one . . . not a look . . . not a word.

Can the nation survive its government and its cities? Yes, because neither is inherently evil. It is only when they are out of the control of the people that they turn an orderly society into an economic and spiritual prison. To right them requires an intensive effort to understand and solve the specific problems that they have created or made worse. It is time to turn to those problems.

35

Foreign Policy
and National Defense

Our foreign policy should be based on the principle that we will go anywhere and do anything that has to be done to protect our citizens from unjust treatment. Our national defense policy should back that up with force.

For Ronald Reagan conquest of other nations is not a proper national goal, and expediency must never be allowed to replace or even temporarily susbtitute for the principle of protection of our citizens.

In Indochina, and before that in Korea, our foreign policy and use of armed forces, and even our explanation of policies to our own people, were based primarily on expediency, on what our leaders thought would have the least disastrous effect on public opinion in the short term. But historically that has not been our policy. Throughout our history, until the waning days of World War II, in instance after instance where the moral principle of right and wrong was at issue, the country never weighed the price.

Let me give an example. In 1853 the United States, then considered by Europe a second-rate military power, stood up to the military might of the Emperor to Austria to save the life of one Hungarian refugee, a man who had taken out only his first citizenship papers and was therefore not even a full-fledged citizen of the United States.

The man's name was Martin Koszta. He had been active in the revolt of the Hungarians against the Emperor of Austria and, when the revolution failed, he fled to America. He took out his first citizenship papers and went into the import business. In July, 1853, he was in the port of Smyrna, in Asiatic Turkey, on business. An Austrian admiral, commanding a large warship in the harbor, heard about Koszta and had him kidnapped, brought to the ship, and clapped in irons. There was no doubt but that the Austrians intended to take him back to Austria and execute him as a revolutionary and a traitor.

But Koszta had a servant who saw the United States flag flying in the harbor from a little war sloop, the U.S.S. *St. Louis.* He went aboard and explained to the commander, Captain Ingraham, what had happened. Ingraham and the servant went to the American consul, who tried to wash his hands of the whole affair when he found out that Koszta had taken out only first citizenship papers. Apparently diplomats were much the same then as now.

Ingraham, however, took a different view of the situation. He reminded the consul that he, Ingraham, was the ranking American officer in the port and that he believed his country had a responsibility to Koszta. He rowed out to the Austrian warship, boarded it, and demanded to see Koszta. The admiral was amused—like most Europeans, he probably believed that they were someday going to recolonize the United States—but he had Koszta brought forth. Ingraham asked him if he wanted the protection of the American flag, and Koszta said that he did. Ingraham promised it to him and rowed back to shore to tell the American consul, who almost collapsed.

When Ingraham returned to the *St. Louis,* he sent one of his lieutenants to the Austrian admiral with the message that any attempt to leave the harbor with Koszta aboard would be resisted with appropriate force and that Ingraham would expect a satisfactory answer about Koszta's fate by 4 o'clock in the afternoon. In the meantime two other Austrian warships had entered the harbor.

As the deadline neared, the crew of the *St. Louis* rolled the cannons into the gunports and lit the tapers. And with that the Austrian ship lowered a boat with Koszta in it, rowed him to shore, and turned him over to the neutral French consul-general. Our Secretary of State eventually negotiated Koszta's release.

After Koszta was safe in French hands, Ingraham wrote a letter of resignation to the Navy, stating that he had acted as he thought his oath of office required, but, if he had embarrassed his country, he would resign. His resignation was turned down on the floor of the Senate with these words: "This battle that was never fought may well turn out to be the most important battle in our nation's history."

Ingraham displayed that combination of pride and humility that can only be motivated in foreign affairs by the honorable principle of protecting the rights of one's fellow citizens. And it's a principle we followed right up to the Yalta Conference in 1945. At least Solzhenitsyn* says that's when we forsook our principles—when we began to sell out the nations of Eastern Europe to the Communists.

A century after Captain Ingraham was praised for winning his battle, General Douglas MacArthur was relieved of his command for insisting upon winning a war.

Korea was our first "no-win" war. We drafted our boys and told them that it was all right to fight and die, but not to fight and die and win, because

---

*Aleksandr I. Solzhenitsyn, Nobel Prize-winning Russian author who spent 10 years in Soviet prisons and is now living in exile in the West.

that might start another war. But when has deciding to settle for a draw ever kept a bully from starting another fight?

Nobody has paid much attention to what General MacArthur said about Korea after he was fired. Everyone remembers the line about "old soldiers never die," but they've forgotten what he prophesied about the effects of our Korean policy. "We shall eventually see the fall of all Indochina to the Communists as a result of our failure in Korea. If we maintain a limited war posture against an enemy willing to fight all out whenever they deem our weakness to be such as to warrant attack, our nation will eventually be isolated." The accuracy of that prophecy and the lack of public recognition of it remind me of Nostradamus, whose first prophecy was that nothing he prophesied would be believed until it had become a fact. We seem to want to worship our heroes without believing them.

But the communists believed him. Korea revealed to the communist world our lack of resolution, so they pushed ahead with their plans in Indochina. Laos was next, in the Kennedy Administration. And the same columnists, the same commentators who had fretted over Chinese involvement in the Korean War cried out about the dangers in Laos: "This would be the wrong war, in the wrong place, at the wrong time." And of course there were dangers, but our indecisive actions only magnified them. In a classic case of interfering in another nation's internal affairs, we forced Laos to set up a coalition government with the communist Pathet Lao. We must have known then, as we know now, that when the communists participate in a coalition government they're going to end up running the show. And we also must have known that, since the Pathet Lao was supported by the North Vietnamese, the next communist move would be in Vietnam. And it was, and the dominoes began to fall—those dominoes so

scorned by the people who were afraid of winning in Korea.

Mention of the Vietnam War triggers a variety of unpleasant responses among Americans. Most of these responses seem to stem from feelings of shame: shame that we were in the war at all, shame that we went about it so clumsily, shame that we were receiving obviously false reports from our own government, shame that we were killing our own soldiers and the Vietnamese for what appeared to be insufficient cause, shame that in the final analysis we lost the war, shame that we were ashamed to admit it. Many people generalized these feelings into one: we had no business intervening in the internal affairs of a small Asian nation.

Reagan disagrees:

I think we were right to be involved. The problems in South Vietnam weren't just internal affairs, and we weren't there because we were imperialistic, as the communists claimed, or altruistic, as we tried to appear. The plain truth of the matter is that we were there to counter the master plan of the communists for world conquest, and it's a lot easier and safer to counter it 8,000 miles away then to wait until they land in Long Beach. We weren't wrong in being there; we were wrong— our government was terribly remiss—in not explaining candidly to the people why we were there. A few experts, in and out of government, wrote books and articles and made speeches explaining the communist threat. But that wasn't the same as the government reporting officially and honestly to the people what we were up against and what was going to be done about it.

The communist master plan, as we know it from published reports, from intelligence sources, and from our own painful experience, is to isolate free nations one by one, stimulating and supplying revolutions without endangering their own troops. What they did in Vietnam was simply to follow the

plan they have pursued in many countries around the world and are pursuing in Portugal and several African and Latin American countries today. I don't think the people of the United States would be so ashamed if they understood the communists' plans; I think they'd be just plain mad. But they'll only understand when the government acknowledges, officially and with supporting facts, that there is a communist plan for world conquest, and that its final step is to conquer the United States.

If our involvement in Vietnam was strategically correct in concept, it was certainly a grim comedy of tactical blunders in operation.

We were involved in a more sensible way under Eisenhower, when we were helping build up South Vietnam to take care of itself. In the late fifties the North Vietnamese weren't ready to admit that the Viet Cong were really North Vietnamese regulars fighting as guerrillas. Kennedy sent in the first troops, and I don't criticize him for that, because I don't know what information he had that the rest of us didn't. I've always held the position that only the one making such a decision can know everything that went into that decision, and perhaps anyone with the same information would have made the same decision. But what I do criticize is what followed from that decision. Having committed combat troops to the field, and having escalated our forces to over half a million soldiers, as Johnson did, we had no moral right to do anything less than defeat the enemy and win the war. Our goal should have been a victory march down the streets of Hanoi.

But what we did instead was to make it impossible for the communists to lose or for us to win. And the communists couldn't help but be aware of it. There they were in a little country that we could have defeated easily, but they could stand up to us because we had told them we weren't going to beat them; we were only going to hold them off. Any time it got too rough for them they could go home, knowing we wouldn't follow. It was a deadly game of tag in which they had a "safe" zone and the South Vietnamese didn't.

The Air Force had a plan at the beginning of the war that would have saved all the bloodshed: a 90-day plan to hit sixty-five targets, all vital to the military, industrial, and transportation capabilities of North Vietnam. At the time the North Vietnamese didn't have antiaircraft missiles and radar to fend off our air attacks. And there would have come a point during those 90 days, as we destroyed their capability to make war, at which they would have given up. But the plan was vetoed in Washington.

Not long ago Breshnev announced an acceleration in Soviet aid for local revolutions, which the communists call "the uprising of the proletariat." Their agents infiltrate worker groups in small nations, stir up people who are already dissatisfied, provide the supplies and propaganda, organize and trigger the revolution, and then sit back and applaud the "spontaneous uprising of the proletariat."

If our people understood their method of operating, if our government documented and presented the facts of case after case of phony revolution fathered by Moscow and Peking, then I believe we could adopt, with the full support of the American people, a policy of beating the communists at their own game. Our policy should be that we are not going to feed our young men into a meat grinder again, any more than the enemy is; that we are going to supply and encourage people in other nations who are not communists, and that we'll use our technological might to keep those nations free; that those free nations will be our allies in what we fully expect will not be a warlike showdown, but a political face-off in which the Soviet Union and the other communist nations will realize that they cannot destroy freedom in the world; that if they push it any farther, they'll have to confront us nose to nose, and that we know they won't do this because they cannot be guaranteed a victory. I believe that we must and can be honest with ourselves, and that the American people will accept and support such candor.

The United States has a tradition of civilian control of the military at the highest levels, in peace and in war. Some observers have accused the military of weakness in planning and execution in Vietnam. Others have tried to pin the blame on civilian advisers. Reagan's opinion: "It was liberal doctrine, and still is. The liberals would have us believe we do not face a threat." His source: Lyndon B. Johnson.

Nancy and I attended the state dinner in Coronado for the outgoing President of Mexico. President Nixon had invited the Johnsons, and Lyndon was Nancy's dinner partner. She asked him what it was like after all those years of public service to return to private life, and he told her there were things he missed and new freedoms he was enjoying. Then he told her that he had a great sense of relief at leaving, because he had lived every moment of his life as president with the fear that he would be responsible for World War III. She asked him if he had any regrets now that it was over. He told her that he'd had two sets of advisers about the Vietnam War; one set wanted him to hold back and not press for victory, while the other set wanted him to be more aggressive. Because of his fear of World War III he had listened to the first set of advisers, but in retrospect his regret was that he had not listened to the second. He was saying after the fact that we should have pursued victory instead of stalemate. And I think

43

that, had we done so, we would have lessened the chances of an eventual World War III.

In addition to sponsoring revolutions, Russia has been steadily overtaking, and even passing, the United States in development of its own armed forces. The threat is clear.

More than 2,000 years ago Demosthenes said to his fellow Athenians, "What sane man would let another man's words rather than his deeds determine whether he is at war or at peace with him?" The Russians can talk peace, but their actions belie the words.

How do you explain in peaceful terms their latest naval maneuvers in every ocean of the world: the greatest naval maneuvers in history, and all offensive in design? They've been increasing their military strength at a rate of 5% per year; ours has been declining by 5% per year. They've built 9,000 new battle tanks while we were building 1,400; they have built 13,300 armored personnel carriers to our 2,500. They have outproduced us nine to one in artillery.

Nor are they ahead only in conventional weapons; they are outstripping us in nuclear weapons as well. Their intercontinental ballistic missiles, like ours, are now being equipped with MIRVs* but their payloads are three to six times greater than ours. We gave away too much in the SALT† agreements because we put no limits on the size of the payload, and yet we knew that they could

---

*Multiple Independent Reentry Vehicles: these are made up of several independently powered warheads attached to one intercontinental ballistic missile. They separate from the ICBM in the upper atmosphere and, under individual power, head for different targets. Thus one ICBM with MIRVs is capable of attacking several targets simultaneously.

†Strategic Arms Limitation Treaty (SALT): agreements between the United States and Russia to limit the operational development and installation of nuclear weapons. The first agreement was signed by both nations October 3, 1972.

carry a larger one. That's always been their strength: bigger engines to carry bigger payloads. We're also getting disturbing reports that they are violating the SALT agreements in ways that we cannot detect with our reconnaissance satellites.

Finally, we know that Russia has quadrupled its espionage and counterintelligence activities related to the United States in just the last couple of years. Yet our own intelligence sources all over the world are drying up because they fear that inevitable leaks from Congressional investigations of the CIA will cost them their lives.

In international confrontations with communist nations we often come out second best and, even when we don't, there are many voices in America that worry more about our victories than our defeats.

The Pueblo case* was a classic example of the folly of our own indecisiveness and the degree to which our people have been misled by the fear of a nuclear war. The communists don't want all-out war, not unless they're guaranteed an absolute victory without much destruction of their own society, a condition that is impossible as long as we are prepared. Yet even today, eight years after the *Pueblo* was captured, some people in this country will think what I'm going to say is jingoistic. How could I think we should risk the possibility of trouble for everyone in order to save eighty-two men? Well, I don't think the risk was nearly as great as the one Captain Ingraham ran in 1853.

The crew of the *Pueblo* was there in our behalf, and suddenly they were prisoners of the North

---

*The U.S.S. *Pueblo* was an American intelligence ship captured in the Sea of Japan by the North Koreans in 1968. The crew was imprisoned in North Korea for 11 months and finally released when a United States negotiator apologized for the violation of North Korea's territorial integrity. The apology was later retracted. North Korea still holds the *Pueblo*.

Koreans. I say the only defensible action, the only moral action, was to move our Seventh Fleet into position outside the harbor and then say to the North Koreans: "Send our ship and our men safely out of that harbor within six hours or we're coming in to get them, and we'll use planes, guns, torpedoes, whatever it takes."

That's how we handled the Mayaquez incident, correctly in my opinion. Yet even when we took a strong and correct stand, the very next day in press conferences I was being asked, with great hostility, if it was worth it to lose more men than we got back. God knows I don't want us to lose anybody. But if we don't stand up for the principle of protecting our citizens and our property, no American will be safe anywhere in the world, including right here in the United States.

Watergate was a disaster to our foreign policy. Richard Nixon had taken us a long way toward a realistic plan for strategic balance with the communists. He was coldly realistic about the Russians. He could meet and confer with them, drink toasts with them. But, unlike the previous leaders we had sent over there, who thought every time the communists smiled they had quit being communists, Nixon never forgot that they were really intent on world domination.

But with Watergate we lost Indochina, and with Indochina we lost our credibility. Not that we have a president who can't be believed, but now no one can be sure that what a president says will be supported by Congress. Certainly Congress has a part to play in foreign policy, in setting overall budgetary restraints and ratifying formal treaties. But if Congress is going to dictate foreign policy to the president, as it did in the War Powers Act, we're in very deep trouble. It's like writing a symphony by committee.

United States strategy in the Middle East is perhaps the prime example of the effects of restrictions in the War

Powers Act placed on the president by Congress as a by-product of Watergate.

Until Indochina blew up and the president was prevented from stopping it by the War Powers Act, we had Israel and the Arabs closer to peace than they'd ever been. One of the great problems of the Middle East situation is that there's so much right on both sides. And Nixon's strategy was brilliant. He had gone a long way toward supplanting Soviet influence in the Arab nations with American influence, but without giving up the support of Israel. His plan was, by being a friend of both, to bring both to the peace table.

But when Congress tied the president's hands with the War Powers Act and the Israelis and Arabs saw the effects in Indochina, they made it clear that they would have a hard time believing that anything an American president told them would be backed up by Congress. And there was no reason related to Watergate for Congress to do what it did in the War Powers Act, except that many congressmen were trying to get at Nixon in any way they could. That act clearly illustrates the shortsightedness and irresponsibility of the Ninety-fourth Congress.

The North Atlantic Treaty Organization (NATO) was set up after World War II as a mutual defense organization of the United States and Europe against the threat of Russian conquest of the West. It survived early crises to become a relatively stable force for peacekeeping in Europe. France dropped out of NATO military affairs in 1966, precipitating continuing questions, here and in Europe, about the necessity or even the desirability of keeping NATO alive.

I think NATO can and must be a key element in our foreign policy and defense structure. There's no way to break up NATO without the strong possibility of losing many countries in it to the influence of the Soviet Union. NATO should be strengthened, but without great added costs to us or its other members. It could benefit from the same reform now going on in our own armed forces—a drastic reduction in the ratio of support forces to combat troops.

I also think it's necessary to get France back into a participating military role in NATO. My understanding is that France's disaffection in 1966 stemmed in large part from being excluded from the control of nuclear weapons. Now, of course, France has developed its own nuclear capability, and I think we ought to recognize it and try to include it in NATO defense forces. France has every reason to be a participant, and we should work to make her change her current position. For a time during the Vietnam War, I almost believed that some of the French were a little jealous of our involvement in Vietnam, having themselves been driven out by the communists in the fifties. Well, if they were, they should be overjoyed now.

As for England, there is a practical thing she could do to greatly increase NATO capability at little cost. With even a fractional postponement of the enormous reduction in the current defense budget, she could arm her submarines with Poseidon missiles, which would produce a weapons' capability equivalent to building more than seventy new submarines.

If we aren't able to keep NATO alive and well, I fear that what some Europeans are predicting will come to pass: that all of Europe and Western Asia will unite in a grand socialist alliance in the next 10 or 15 years and become the largest power block in history. The people who are predicting this are not necessarily saying that it's desirable, but that it's inevitable. And that, of course, is nothing more than confirmation of Karl Marx's theory of the inevitability of socialism: that the people will simply give in to the idea that socialism must happen. It's a frightening thought, but it should make Americans all the more determined to show Europe that we have no intention of leaving the pages of history with a whimper: that, with or without them, we'll make our stand.

The only people I have met recently who are not confused about what our foreign and defense policies should be are the men who were prisoners of war in North Vietnam. They had a duty and they did it, in the most difficult circumstances imaginable. Nancy and I entertained some of them at our home, and another guest asked them why they had endured the torture—why they had not given in in the beginning and saved themselves the pain. The men looked at him as if he were out of his mind, and one of them said simply, "We were prisoners. The only thing left that we could do for our country was to hold out as long as possible." That's the sense of duty that we have to recapture.

Churchill summed it up for the British when Czechoslovakia fell to the Nazis at the beginning of World War II. "This is only the beginning of the reckoning. This is only the first sip, the first foretaste of the bitter cup which will be proferred to us year by year, unless by a supreme recovery of moral health and martial vigor we rise again and take our stand for freedom as in the olden times." His words are now our destiny.

Inflation, Recession, and Government Spending

The United States has experienced two economic recessions in the past six years: the first relatively mild, the second much more severe.

Recessions are only the pockmarks that come from the disease. The disease is inflation. We can go on putting calamine lotion on the pockmarks, but we'd be a lot better off if we concentrated on curing the disease.

In 1969 inflation was at 6%, and we fought it down to 2.7%. Then came the pressure from Congress and organized labor because of slightly increased unemployment. It was a small recession and a small price to pay for an end of inflation, but it apparently was too expensive politically. Well, we cured the recession and we seemed to become prosperous again. Everything was going great, except that in the next three years inflation climbed to between 12% and 14%. We cut it in half again, brought it back down to between 6% and 7%. This time, however, the recession was about twice as bad as the first time. Now Alan Greenspan, the president's chief economic adviser, says we're recovering nicely, more slowly than we'd hoped but nicely, and that we can probably count on renewed prosperity. But inflation has started to rise again. How high will it go this time? 20%? 24%? And when we start to fight it, which I assume will be after the national election, will the recession be twice as bad as the last one? How many doublings of inflation and recession before we reach full-scale depression?

For 35 years American public education has indoctrinated American youth in the belief that another severe depression is impossible. Supposedly the New Deal legislation of the thirties depression-proofed the country by providing adequate federal insurance against economic disasters, large or small.

I don't think so. It would be wonderful to know there could never again be a national depression, but I don't think we really can know that. We've done a lot of things to help stave off depression. Redistribution of income has widened purchasing power. There's bank deposit insurance, but what would happen if there were a run on the banks? The government hasn't enough money to pay off that insurance. It may be more difficult to get into a depression, but the inflationary pattern we've established could well end in depression.

Inflation is a cruel and deceptive "disease." Although prices rise, so do wages, leading many people to believe they are becoming more prosperous. But inevitably prices outrun wages, and the extra money in people's pockets won't buy as much as it could before. Why do prices rise? A major reason is the federal creation of "inflationary money."

When the federal government runs a big deficit, as it's doing now, it has to borrow the money to make up the difference. When normal borrowing won't cover the whole deficit, the Federal Reserve Board "prints" new money by creating deposits in federal reserve banks for the government to borrow. That money is purely inflationary money, because it is unearned money. It isn't the result of increased production of goods and services; it is just "printed" to loan to the federal government. An increase in the money supply not matched by a comparable increase in goods and services lowers the value of the money, and as a result prices rise.

In 1946 the money supply was $110 billion, and a dollar was, by definition, worth a dollar. In 1974 the money supply was $283.4 billion, but the same dollar was worth only 38.8 cents. In terms of actual purchasing power—the ability of people to buy the things they need—there was no more real money available in 1974 than in 1946.

Government controls the economy, and the bureaucracy controls the government and has since the days of Franklin Roosevelt. If you read Rexford Tugwell, who was one of Roosevelt's chief advisers, you find that Roosevelt was often poorly informed of his advisers' plans until they were implemented, because they were so different from his campaign promises and apparently from his beliefs. His advisers wanted to imitate the fascism of Mussolini in Italy—to pull the control of the economy into central government. I believe that Roosevelt started out with the idea of licking the Depression through temporary government programs, and it was only gradually that his advisers weaned him into support of a permanent and omnipotent federal bureaucracy.

Protection of the interests of the people against the whims of the bureaucracy should be one of the top priorities of our elected representatives in Congress.

Not only do congressmen seldom realize what the bureaucracy is doing to them, they're even afraid to go against some of the agencies and bureaus. They're more afraid of the bureaucrats than of their own constituents back home, because their constituents have even less information than they do. The bureaucracy has the information and guards it jealously; it can cut a congressman off at the knees if it gets mad at him—make him the laughing stock of Washington.

Anyone who touches a nerve in the bureaucracy can expect retaliation. Several times I've challenged bureaucratic methods—the Department of Labor's method of determining who is unemployed, for instance. Invariably an article will appear within a few weeks refuting, with elaborate analysis, what I said. The article doesn't mention me and doesn't say it's a refutation, but that is obviously its purpose and thrust. It used to bother me; I'd wonder if I'd been wrong. But then I found out that, no, I hadn't been wrong; I'd been a target of the bureaucracy, which uses as weapons statistics that are contrived and often unreliable. Disraeli said, "There are lies, damned lies, and statistics!" The bureaucracy prefers statistics.

The only thing that's going to curb inflation with any lasting effect is to reduce the long-term growth of the money supply. That means slowing the growth of government spending, forcing government to grow no faster than the economy, and preferably even a little slower.

The public has often been misled about federal budget cutting. They've been conditioned to think of a budget cut as a reduction from the amount of money spent the previous year. But the federal budget has been growing at the rate of $40 billion a year. All of the budget cuts that have been proposed in the last few years, by me and by other people, are either reductions in the rate of growth or transfers of federal programs to the states. If the people realized that, I believe they would be less concerned about whether a "cut-back" federal government could meet its obligations.

It's time the people realize that our federal government is financially out of control. Special interests fatten themselves on our taxes while we cannot keep up with an inflation caused by the

53

federal government spending money it doesn't have.

An example of the ways in which Americans are misled about taxes and government spending is the constant appeal by the liberals for more business taxes. Every business tax, without exception, must be included in the price of products. Businesses don't pay taxes; they collect taxes for the government from you and me. We haven't always been so blind to that fact. In 1942 the AFL demanded that the federal government cancel the capital gains tax because "this tax is making it difficult for business to expand and provide jobs our people need." We are one of the few countries in the world to have such a tax—a tax that directly impedes real economic growth. The AFL was smart enough to see it then; why can't they see it now?

The best way to control federal spending is to control federal revenues and the ability of the federal government to deficit spend: in effect to restore to the people control over how much of their income the government can take and spend. That could be accomplished by a constitutional amendment to prohibit further deficit spending and limit, except in time of national emergency, the percentage of the nation's personal income that could be taken as revenue by the federal government. Similar amendments could be adopted by each state to prevent the federal government from forcing higher costs on state and local governments.

The rate of growth of government would then be no greater than the rate of growth of the economy as a whole, and the progress toward state socialism would be halted. The effects would be felt gradually as the government was forced to exercise more care in assessing and establishing priorities for the expenditure of limited funds. There would be no more innocuous bills passed that ended up three or four years later costing hundreds of millions of dollars.

The bureaucrats would oppose any limitation, as would those who believe that the only way to salvation is complete government control of our lives and property. That's why the limitation would be most effective if it were constitutional. Congress has made previous attempts to limit spending and the national debt, but those limits have never lasted more than a year. Of course, getting Congress to limit its own spending is like trying to get an alcoholic to limit himself to one drink a day.

One indicator of the fiscal irresponsibility of the federal government is the national debt: the amount of money the government has had to borrow because it budgeted to spend more money than it received in revenues. The national debt has just climbed past $600 billion, with a deficit this year of more than $60 billion. The debt has doubled since 1960. Long a matter of public concern, the debt now seems to have become so large that the public is inured to its continued growth.

We used to be able to reduce the national debt. We accumulated a debt of almost $25 billion during World War I and were systematically repaying it until the early thirties. Then the debt started to climb and hasn't stopped since. There are two ways to reduce it. You can start paying it off, and we should do that. But more importantly we should make sure it doesn't get any bigger. That in itself is a kind of reduction because, as the gross national product grows, the national debt shrinks as a percentage of it. Although the dollar amount of the debt stays the same, the burden of it is less in a larger economy.

We need to reduce the absolute dollar value of the debt because of the enormous interest that's now being paid on it. The government pays out about $30 billion a year in interest. If we could reduce the national debt by $8 billion a year, which is less than 2.5% of our $350 billion budget, we'd save almost $4 billion dollars in future interest payments.

The main reason we don't reduce the national debt, the main reason we have government-produced inflation, is that no politician can stand up to an increase in unemployment.

The Nobel prize-winning economist, Friedrich Hayek, indicated in early 1975 that only several months of 13% to 14% unemployment would halt the inflationary growth in the United States and that, the longer inflation continued, the higher the rates of unemployment and the longer the periods of time that would be required to stop it. Hayek expressed doubt that America could bring itself to accept such unemployment and predicted, therefore, that the most likely course of the economy would be spiraling inflation leading to nationalization of industry and eventually to economic collapse.

Several economists—hard-headed ones who aren't afraid to draw unpopular conclusions from logic and history—have said that higher unemployment is the necessary evil we must face if we are going to stop inflation. If it is, and if the American people know the situation and the alternatives, I'm confident they will be able to bear the burden. There's nothing wrong with bearing a burden if all of us share in it.

In a time of rising unemployment, the problem is not only the people who are unemployed. It's also all those people who go to work each morning wondering, "Am I next?" Now if they knew that even if they are laid off, they're not going to starve, that they're going to get their jobs back after a few months, and that the alternative is eventually having to take bushel baskets of money to the store to buy bread, and then finding no bread at all, I know the American people will make the short-term sacrifice. But they won't if their leaders don't explain the situation clearly and honestly. We had that problem with the energy crisis: the people were convinced it was nothing but a plot to raise gasoline and fuel oil prices.

In the most recent recession some smaller companies, usually at the insistence of the workers, put everyone on a shorter work week and cut their pay instead of laying anyone off. Working through the problem this way requires that both government and business take the workers into their confidence, involve them in the decisions, and rely on their ability and willingness to share in making the solution as painless as possible.

We have to be able to accept that unemployment is going to rise before we can get over the disease of inflation. To pretend it isn't going to rise is like trying to ignore the fever by breaking the thermometer.

The government has abundantly padded many Americans against the unpleasantness of recession, which may be why in the most recent recession the inflation rate didn't fall below 6%.

It was hard to find the signs of recession, at least after the first few weeks. The resorts were crowded; the parking lots and highways were crowded. There were virtually no signs of hard times to those of us who had lived through the Depression. I don't mean that no one was hurt. It's a traumatic thing to be without a job and need and want one. But when you read that 50,000 of the laid-off Michigan auto workers had their unemployment checks sent to them in Florida all winter, you begin to wonder how much great distress there was.

Retail sales recovered quickly. Restaurants were crowded. In Hawaii many were unemployed and seeking work through the employment agencies. When the federal government extended the period of unemployment pay to a full year, it was reported that the lines at the employment agencies disappeared. There was no need to come around for another six months.

If government controls the economy and also is the principal cause of its problems, who will provide the leadership to solve those problems? Two sources come immediately to mind—business and labor. Are both already tied too closely to government? Dwight Eisenhower left the presidency in 1960 with a warning about the dangers of a military-industrial complex.

He gave a warning, but it was not, as many anti-defense militants have tried to convince the people, a warning that there was already a dangerous military-industrial complex preying on the people. In the full context of his remarks he was warning that such a power complex was something we had to be careful to avoid because other countries had been taken over by just such forces. He was telling us that we needed a strong defense, so strong that no potential aggressor would be willing to risk destruction to conquer us. But at the same time we must make sure that we are not conquered some day by our own defense establishment.

Since Eisenhower's warning the defense budget has more than doubled but, as a percentage of the total federal budget, it has shrunk from 48% to 27%. During the same period the defense budget has also shrunk as a percentage of the gross national product from 8.7% to 5.5%. Other expenditures, however, have caused the total government to take an ever-increasing share of the gross national product, and many Americans feel squeezed between big government, big business, and big labor.

Business and labor have both gone to Washington too often for favors. George Meany once told me that he had argued with Walter Reuther over some of the labor advantages Reuther was seeking from Congress. Meany thought those advantages should be negotiated with management. But Reuther's atti-

tude was, "Why bother when we can get them from Congress?"

And there's no question but that business short-sightedly has sought regulations that appear to favor it. When such a beneficent protector as the government is willing, business is not above seeking its help in curbing possible competition. The dairy industry put itself in the hands of government and found that, through governmental price-fixing, the incompetents in the industry were kept in business, to the detriment of everyone.

Once a business puts itself in the hands of government, however, it stops being an influence. Government controls it, and a beggar doesn't have many choices. I think big business itself is now beginning to realize that every time it tries to influence government it ends up, hat in hand, begging favors. My plea to businessmen is to start fighting back to the free enterprise system. It seems that in their rush to Washington they've almost forgotten that the economic basis of this country is capitalism.

The problem with labor too is big government. Some months ago I received a letter from a union member complaining because he couldn't vote secretly in an important union election, an election to decide whether or not a large amount of the members' dues would be sent to the national treasury. For eight years I fought in California to require that union elections be secret. But the state AFL-CIO controlled the votes of the Democratic majority in the legislature, and the law was never passed. Obviously the big union leaders still value their ability to influence government. The move to stop government growth must come from the rank and file union members. Recent polls indicate that the members are beginning to view their own leadership just as they view government: too powerful. One poll last year indicated that a majority of union members even support right to work laws.

Small business is the strongest antigovernment growth force. After years of treating small businesses as rivals to be bought out or forced out, the big corporations are just beginning to discover that the hundreds of thousands of individual entrepreneurs who run their own businesses, meet their own payrolls, and work in their own plants, are the real capitalists in America.

Do we or do we not believe in government by the people? The citizens of America are ready for leadership that will speak to them directly. They're fed up with inflation and with big government, and they sense that there's a definite relationship between the two. We must have leadership that will go over the heads of the bureaucrats, the Congress, the favor-seeking business and union leaders: leadership that will speak directly to the people, tell them honestly what the economic problems are and what must be done to solve them. Journalists can't make that contact; neither can economists or teachers. It must come from the President.

Education

Public education in the United States was founded on the belief that there can be no government by the people unless there are literate people.

In the past 20 years there has been a steadily growing public dissatisfaction with public education, a dissatisfaction that can be related directly to the cost, performance, and atmosphere of the public education system. Costs per student have grown far faster than the cost of living; scores on standard achievement tests have dropped; behavior and discipline problems have multiplied until, for many children and teachers, physical fear is an every-school day experience. Despite the application of an abundance of financial and intellectual resources to the problems, public schools continue to worsen.

Public education has deteriorated at the same time policy and decision-making power were being centralized in state and federal governments. How and to what extent does the centralization of school authority improve or decrease the ability of public schools to meet public needs? Reagan's answer starts from an understanding of what public education was intended to do and the ways in which it has developed.

We developed public education so that people would be able to read and understand the public issues, vote intelligently, and make informed decisions about the relationship between themselves and their government. In the early days higher

61

education was mainly for the affluent because it was offered only in the prestigious universities and colleges built with private money. We created state universities to provide for those who couldn't afford the private schools, and since we couldn't afford to staff the public elementary and high schools with Yale and Harvard graduates, we set up public state teachers' colleges. The purpose of public higher education was to provide a less expensive version of what Yale and Harvard were doing.

But we lost sight of that purpose and allowed our public universities and colleges to begin competing with private schools to see who could spend the most money. Today I doubt if there's a private university in the country that can match the luxury in facilities and curriculum found in most of our public institutions.

A few years ago I visited the theater arts department in a California state college. The college is located in a rural area, and not many people seriously interested in a career in theater, movies, or television would choose to go there. Yet the facilities, built at taxpayers' expense, were so elaborate that if any of the graduates ever did succeed, they would never perform in facilities up to the quality in which they had been trained.

In my first year as governor of California I criticized the University of California for what I called "subsidizing intellectual curiosity." And I was really raked over the coals for that. People thought I was anti-intellectual, a real Neanderthal man. What I thought then and think now is that public higher education should contribute to the public welfare. There are many courses in our public universities that can only be described as educational luxury. Students who want to take them should be able to, but not by means of a public subsidy. We also have "professional students," people who don't want to leave the campus atmosphere and who just go on year after year taking all the courses the university offers. Should support for that kind of student be a public responsibility? Why should a truck driver worried about putting his own kids through school be taxed to provide a hobby-type education to someone else's kids?

I'm not anti-intellectual, and I know there are gray areas to this problem. One of the great faults of both conservatives and liberals is the desire to draw a sharp line on every issue, and this is one where a sharp line can't be drawn. But I believe it's clear we've gone too far in burdening the taxpayers with costs they shouldn't have to bear for public higher education.

The next step in the process of increasing governmental control of higher education was the introduction of federal grants to both public and private institutions of higher learning.

There were a great many educators and college administrators who were fearful that federal grants would mean federal interference, which we'd always been free of in this country. A group of university presidents went to Washington to voice their fear. They proposed that the federal government, instead of distributing grants, allow a $100 tax credit to any taxpayer who wished to contribute to an educational institution. They were willing to compete for $100 contributions rather than take large federal grants at the risk of government control. But the federal director of education rejected the idea, telling them that with such a plan the federal government would not be able to realize its "social objectives."

I would like to know who gave the federal government the right to establish social objectives in higher education. But if one of the objectives was to still all opposition, it has certainly succeeded. One college president told me that when the group was being organized to go to Washington, federal grants had already reached the size that some presidents did not dare to be associated with a complaint about them. I don't know how much greater an influence government can have on higher education than to make college presidents afraid to state their own minds, and I would guess that you couldn't find a dozen such presidents who would feel free to criticize the federal grant system today.

The fiscal year 1976 federal budget for higher education is more than $7.4 billion.

No matter how much the bureaucrats deny it, the purse strings always end up manipulating the policy.

The question of the growing costs of education below the university level should most appropriately be focused on whether or not higher expenditures produce better education.

California has a classic example of the impact of spending on educational quality. San Francisco spends almost twice as much per student as Los Angeles. Both cities have similar problems, yet Los Angeles' students score consistently higher than those in San Francisco. San Francisco's performance in public education is close to the worst in the state. Obviously, money is not the answer to quality education.

An important factor in the relationship of spending to quality is the way school boards are set up. Until recently, San Francisco's school boards were politically appointed, not elected, and it's hardly a coincidence that San Francisco's school system is top heavy with administrators. All over the country we see the greatest relative cost increases in additions of nonteaching personnel, much more so than in numbers of teachers. We've made stifling bureaucracies of our schools, to the detriment of teachers and students.

And we've done virtually nothing to instill in our kids the kind of respect for home, school, and country that would end violence in the classroom and corridors. In fact, the prevailing theories about patriotism in the past 30 years have probably caused some of the violence in schools. After World War II our educators apparently decided that succeeding generations should be patriots only of the world and not of the nation. Saluting the flag, learning and understanding the protocol associated with the national anthem, feelings of devotion to home, community, school, church, or nation have been downplayed more and more each year in our schools. Actually, there has been a concerted effort to debunk the kind of patriotism that we used to have. Our patriots are presented in their seamiest aspects. It's healthy to study thoroughly a national hero, warts and all, but when the warts are enlarged to cover up the good deeds that made the person a hero, then we've gone beyond objectivity into unjustifiable cynicism.

Courts in the past several years have addressed the question of whether educational opportunity is affected by the spending capability of school districts, which in turn is directly dependent on taxing capability and, indirectly, on district wealth. The most significant cases have been *Rodriquez* in Texas and *Serrano* in California.

There are two issues of importance in these cases. The first is whether the parents in a poor district should be penalized by living in an area that cannot afford an education that would enable their children to get into a university. I think that even the most devoted advocates of local control would agree that such a penalty would be unfair, and that a statewide floor of school support should be guaranteed, whatever the fiscal resources of the individual district. We must remember, however, that spending doesn't produce education and the floor of support doesn't need to be set at the level of the most spendthrift district. A floor of support should be just that, a floor.

The other issue is the more dangerous one. What is apparently being sought by the plaintiffs is a ruling that local districts cannot supplement the floor with their own resources, even if they want to. This is socialism with a vengeance. And of course state legislatures have never ceased to do foolish things on the basis of the state aid that's provided to local districts. Frankly, I can't see what business it is of a state or a district if another district wants to tax itself more heavily to provide some enhancement to its schools.

Teachers and school administrators know from long and often sad experience that public interest in public education is highly erratic. A few parents show persistent interest, and many parents get involved, intensively but haphazardly, on specific issues. Nonparents are generally most concerned about school taxes. The result is a highly uneven level of input from the public as to how public education should be conducted.

In the last school board election in Los Angeles, only 30% of the electorate turned out. I remember a special election in another city in which only 7% of the people voted to fill a vacancy on the school board. I don't know of anything that people are more concerned about than the education of their children. Yet nobody votes.

The major reason for voter apathy is the anonymity of the school board and its members in a large district. In a city the size of Los Angeles, with one district for all the elementary schools, a voter can hardly be familiar with the names of school board members, let alone know their impact as individuals on school policies. And with textbooks selected by the state, and a State Superintendent of Public Instruction laying down regulations about curriculum, method, and teacher qualifications, it's no wonder most voters feel their votes are meaningless.

Several years ago the Coleman Report on education set the maximum size for an efficient school district at 20,000 students. If the district included both grade schools and high schools, this would mean a district for every 100,000 to 150,000 people. I think that number is far too high for most cities and states. But many states, with the encouragement of the federal government and the insistence of the National Education Association, have been trying to reduce the number of districts in the name of "economies of scale." They claim that it costs less per student to run a larger district.

Even if the cost were the most important factor in education, which it isn't, it would be foolish to make bigger and bigger school districts. There are no economies of scale to be obtained in a labor-intensive public service like education. The more students, the more teachers. And the more teachers there are in a given district, the more supervisors that can be justified. And if they can be justified, you can bet they'll be hired. In large districts, the number of supervisors grows proportionately faster than the number of students.

The National Education Association (NEA), a national quasi-union of teachers, has advocated school district consolidation, even to the extent of multistate districts.

The movement toward centralization through larger and larger school districts is not new. One NEA official said some years ago that "Just as the states have found that the individual school district is an anachronism out of the past, no longer practical, so have we learned that 50 different state educational systems are impractical." The first half of that statement is untrue, and the second half is self-serving. What the NEA leadership wants is a national education system, controlled from Washington. But the farther we have gone toward centralization, the worse has been the performance of public education.

That doesn't seem to bother the NEA. They boast

that they can raise more money than COPE* to elect to public office people who think their way. They're more interested in lobbying and nest-feathering than in education. They appeal to an individual teacher's desire to be a professional at the same time they are seeking to remove all possibilities of professionalism through their advocacy of a national school system.

There are a great many teachers, members of NEA and its state affiliates, who don't agree with its philosophy and goals at all. Many of them come up to me at public meetings. They look over both shoulders, then lower their voices and tell me what they really think. Here they are, dues-paying members, and they are afraid to express their opposition, afraid of what their peers and their administrators will think of them. I think its pretty lousy when we allow an organization to foster that attitude among our teachers, who should be the seekers after truth.

I've always been opposed to monopoly, always believed that monopoly is evil. I don't care whether it's corporate monopoly, or government monopoly, or labor monopoly, it's monopoly that's evil, not who's doing it. Right now in public education we are very close to a monopoly. Every year thousands of parochial and private schools close down because they can't compete against the public schools, which drain off more and more in taxes. Most of us are left with no choice but the public schools, good or bad. And most of us have no control over whether those schools are good or bad.

The loss of citizen control of public schools in the face of increased centralization has been accomplished by a growing distance between the way many teachers teach and the way parents want them to. The prevailing method of public school instruction, from preschool to graduate

*Coalition of Public Employee Organizations, a recent and loose-knit alliance apparently for the purpose of influencing legislators and elections.

school, has become a combination of force-feeding and indoctrination. Parents are astonished to find their children have been exposed to only one point of view on important issues; students are appalled to find that their grades depend more on agreement with their teachers' viewpoints than on knowledge of the facts. Moreover, the viewpoints of the teachers most oriented to indoctrination seem to be consistently socialistic and authoritarian, anticapitalistic and antidemocratic.

I'm convinced that some years ago educational reformers decided to invade the teacher's colleges, to start turning out crops of teachers imbued with their philosophy.

As governor of California, I sat on the Board of Regents of the University of California. When I offered some complaints about the obvious liberal bias and indoctrination by the faculty, there were immediate screams that I was trying to inject politics into education. What I was really trying to do was take politics out of education, my politics and everyone else's. What I said at a Regents' meeting was, "I would be as opposed to having my own philosophy imposed on these young people as I am at having liberal doctrine imposed on them." The press carefully refrained from quoting me.

The dangers of indoctrination to a democracy are obvious. All healthy kids rebel at some time and in some degree against the ideas and authority of their parents. And that rebellion almost always takes place during schooling. Indoctrination then, at the hands of a fascinating teacher, can destroy the values instilled over years by the parents. I don't believe a teacher has any right to indoctrinate students to his point of view, no matter what it is. We must return to the traditional ethics that kept a teacher or professor from expressing his personal views on an issue or idea unless at the same time he told his students where to find the opposite opinion. That's how it was when I was in school, but when you tell kids today that's how it was, they stare at you in disbelief.

The answer to the problems of public education, I believe, is a return to the neighborhood school. There are those who say it didn't work, but in the last 25 years we've added more to the total sum of man's knowledge than in all of preceding history, and a large part of that addition was produced by Americans, educated in neighborhood grade and high schools. What was wrong with that school system?

Some say neighborhood schools won't work in a large city and point to the failures in New York City. But there were some successes in that hurried experiment in New York, despite almost unbelievable pressures from the teachers' union.

The opponents of neighborhood schools have two arguments, neither of which has much to do with educational quality. The first is that a large district is more efficient to operate, and we know that's nonsense. The second is that many neighborhoods don't have the wealth to support quality schools without outside help. Well, that's easy to solve—establish a broad-based fund-raising district for tax collection and distribution. But don't give that large fund-raising district any control over how the schools are going to be run; limit it to distributing money on a per-student basis.

Then let the people decide on the number, size, and location of school districts within a fund-raising district. Only the people who live in a neighborhood know its boundaries. And I'm convinced that most of the districts formed would be neighborhood districts, with perhaps one high school and two or three grade schools, or even smaller. Small enough that all of the people would know the members of the school board they elect. Small enough that if a kid's causing trouble in school, he's not anonymous, and neither are his parents. Small enough that parents would not be intimidated by teachers who don't want them to have any input to the education of their children. Small enough that teachers could count on the support of the parents in discipline, homework, and the needs of the school that can't be met by dollars. Small enough that, if the voters of the district choose to raise their own taxes to supplement the money from the fund-raising district, they'll know what they're buying with those taxes.

Neighborhood schools would be the most effective deterrent to the policies of the NEA and others who seek to force upon us the intellectual sterility of a national school system. Teachers talk about academic freedom, but they usually seem to mean freedom only for them to determine what and how they're going to teach. What about the educational freedom of the parent who's forced by law to send his child to school? What about the educational freedom of the student? Neighborhood schools serve all three. The only people they don't serve are the bureaucrats and union leaders.

I owe a lot to public education, as do most Americans. When I was a kid, I was an avid reader, always at the library, finishing at least one or two books every week. I thought I was doing that on my own, but now I know that somewhere along the line that urge to learn was stimulated by school, as well as home.

The problem today is not that we're under-educating or neglecting students as much as it is that we're spoon feeding them, indoctrinating them to the point that once they leave school, for the day or for life, they feel no obligation to acquire more knowledge. Only later do they understand that they missed something, which is why adult education is now so much in demand, to the chagrin of the professional educators. Teachers must return to the precept that their job is to teach how to think, not what to think!

71

Work

My first summer job, when I was 14 years old, was for an outfit that bought up old houses and remodeled them. I started in digging foundations and hauling away debris, but before the summer was over I had laid hardwood floor, painted houses—everything that had to be done to remodel a place. At the end of each week the boss reached in his pocket and paid me in cash. He didn't have to keep records of my hours, pay withholding and Social Security taxes for me, or provide workmen's compensation, health and life insurance, coffee breaks, and sterilized paper towels. The only person he had to pay for my labor was me, and that made me worth it to him.

A teen-ager cannot find such a job today. A myriad of federal and state regulations prevent the kind of informal employer-employee relationship Reagan enjoyed. Some of the regulations prevent teen-age employment in the name of safety.

When I was governor, there was a frost in the Berkeley Hills of California, which killed many eucalyptus trees. The trees had to be cut down quickly, since the longer they stood there, the greater the fire danger and the tougher they would be to cut down. I suggested to the mayors of Berkeley and other communities involved that they set up a summer program for their teen-agers to cut down and remove the trees. They told me that under the laws tractors and chainsaws were hazardous tools; that they couldn't allow teen-agers to use them.

I've seen 12-year-old farm kids who drive tractors and operate chainsaws better than most adults. The government's forcing us to wet-nurse these kids who, before we became so citified, did all of the jobs around farms and homes as a matter of course.

Tax and insurance laws usually make it uneconomical to hire teen-agers for part-time work.

Not too long ago a storekeeper would just stop a kid going by his store and ask him if he wanted to make a couple of bucks. If the kid said "yes," the storekeeper would hand him a broom and show him where to sweep. Both of them benefited. But that can't be done anymore. The storekeeper waits until he has enough work for a full-time employee and hires an adult. That's why teen-age unemployment is so high. What's more, as these teen-agers grow older, they'll still be unemployed because they've never been given a chance to learn how to do a job.

I've had groups of teen-agers beg me to become a spokesman for them in an attempt to get the government tax and minimum wage laws waived for them. They're not demanding $2.25 an hour. They'd be happy to work for whatever a job is worth. I can't believe it's impossible to waive those laws and also build in protection so that cheap-minded employers can't take advantage of the teen-agers. That's what government's for.

Not only are America's teen-agers denied the on-the-job training opportunities of previous generations, they are also woefully undereducated in the economic principles that will affect their working lives. The basic economics of the business world have been virtually ignored by the

73

public education system for the past 40 years. In fact, many educators consider business to be anti-intellectual and not worthy of study.

I think it's the other way around. Business isn't anti-intellectual; the intellectuals for some time have been antibusiness. They're more than willing to take the money business makes for university endowments and research grants. But if a businessman wants to suggest how his money might be used, he's violating "academic freedom." How gauche and uncivilized of him! The fact is that business today is pretty civilized, and even the businessmen who came up from the assembly line are apt to have MBAs from Harvard. They know the problems of education and what's missing in the people they hire. They deserve to be listened to by the so-called intellectuals.

There are a few economic educational programs for teen-agers. One of them is the Junior Achievement Program, sponsored by businessmen, where the kids are taught about business the practical way—by engaging in it. The kids, in groups, develop ideas for products, and then actually make and sell the products. They learn from experience the relationship between investment and profit. Some are very successful; some aren't. But they all learn.

Everybody should learn basic economies because everybody is really in business for profit. The worker's wages must pay for the absolute necessities of life for him and his family. Anything he makes above that is profit, which he can invest or spend for entertainment or luxuries. That's all profit is to a business owner. He must take in enough income to pay the necessities: costs of labor, shop maintenance, power, and materials. And he must pay for the necessities of life for himself and his family. What's left over for pleasure or investment is his profit.

Few people work for themselves, and the number who do has dwindled steadily throughout the twentieth century. Perhaps of more significance is the ever-increasing percentage of workers who don't and can't even know the people they work for.

Impersonality may well be the biggest problem in today's working world. Seventy-five years ago the person who owned the factory also ran it. When he talked to his employees he was the owner, the manager, the boss. In today's large corporations the management hierarchy is only employees, too. The corporation is impersonally owned by millions of people, as well as foundations, churches, and even labor unions.

Nowadays there's a management "profession." These professional managers' primary concern is convincing a board of directors, which generally reflects the opinions of a majority of the stockholders, that they—the managers—are doing a good job of raising the volume of sales and lowering the costs of production. Few of them realize that, to the average worker on the production line, the corporation president, whom he's probably never seen, is the boss, the owner. And of course the president is making decisions based on the pressure he's getting from his employers, who in turn only represent the owners.

The same kind of management hierarchy, which is really just another bureaucracy, exists in the large labor unions. Unions are big business now, and the union president is no longer a machine worker who was just elected president by his fellow workers. The union hierarchy has its share of Harvard MBAs to handle pension funds and tax problems. They have to justify their existence, as all bureaucracies do, and they do it with a constant barrage of propaganda to convince the workers that the "boss" is the enemy. The "boss" may well include the union itself, which may have invested its pension funds in company stock. But the effect of

the propaganda on the workers is to drain away their pride in where they work and what they produce. They begin to think that somehow they're getting even with the "boss" by slowing down production or making defective products.

For eight years I emceed the G.E. Theater on television, and part of my job was to tour General Electric plants throughout the United States to talk to the employees and see how they made G.E. products. I'll never forget my great surprise at how much money management spends to persuade the workers to make the product right.

At the refrigerator plant in Louisville, Kentucky, I walked 46 miles of assembly line twice—once for the day shift and once for the night shift—to meet all of the employees individually as they worked at their machines. Every morning I'd start where I'd left off the day before. After dinner I'd come back and do the swing shift. I was there a week.

I came to one point near the end of the assembly line where the refrigerators were proceeding along a track, and there was a spur track running off to one side through some swinging doors. All of a sudden two guys in white coats came out of the swinging doors and grabbed a couple of refrigerators at random off the line and pushed them down the spur track through the swinging doors. From all the workers in the area came a loud "boo," maybe partially good-natured, maybe not.

The fellows in the white coats were the testers, and their job was to pick refrigerators at random and put them through the toughest tests imaginable. For example, to test the door latch they had a machine that would open and close the door, over and over again, day and night, while the back was off the refrigerator so they could see how long the light kept going on and off as the door was opened and closed. I asked them what service life the tests were predicated on and they told me 25 years' normal operation.

I thought that was kind of self-defeating—if they

were making machines to last 25 years and everyone bought one, they'd be out of business. They explained to me that business doesn't work that way, that there are always people who want new styles and new features and other people who'll buy the used machines. But all over the plant, besides the various test laboratories, there were enormous signs that read: "Would you buy it yourself?" or "Your neighbor may buy this." All this was to insure that a worker would not get careless and would have the same interest in seeing that every refrigerator coming off the line was capable of 25 years of normal abuse.

I think Ralph Nader is as phony as a $3 bill when he acts as if the companies making the products are purposely trying to shortchange the customers by making things that don't work. If you analyze it, that charge is ridiculous on the face of it.

Take the person who buys a lemon of an automobile. He gets mad at the car and mad at the company. But if he stops to think, he realizes that everyone else he sees who has the same make and model is satisfied. His lemon can't be a contrivance of management. It certainly wasn't the management that said, "Let's turn out a bad car here and there." Some worker let something slip. Maybe he'd had a fight with his wife or maybe he'd stayed up too late and had a hangover . . . but something didn't get tightened right or ground down to the right tolerance and the result was a car that gave its owner continued trouble.

I've never heard Mr. Nader talk about worker carelessness. He wants to blame everything on top management, even when it doesn't make sense to do so. But one reason the blame is levied and believed is the impersonality of the large corporations.

For 50 years labor unions have been the dominant force in defining the conditions and rewards of work in the United States. That period has been one of almost continuous inflation. Although the unions have consistently denounced inflation, the positions of their leaders on economic problems have usually encouraged the deficit spending and government growth that have produced inflation.

When George Meany testifies to Congress that this country can afford a $100 billion deficit to solve the unemployment problem, it's obvious that he's been the victim of bad advice. If we overspend by $100 billion now, he'll be back asking that we overspend by $250 billion the next time. When government uses a deficit to create work, it also creates inflation.

When I was president of the Screen Actors' Guild, I represented 31 local unions in testimony before the Ways and Means Committee of Congress. These unions had picked me to go to Washington to endorse a certain tax reform measure. When I got to Washington, I was handed a book containing the AFL-CIO tax policy for that year, and it was directly opposite to the position I had been selected to represent. The book called for a $12 billion tax increase, because the socialistically inclined economists at AFL-CIO headquarters had defined $12 billion dollars worth of social reforms they wanted the government to adopt. That's how organized big labor arrives at its policy positions. The workers have little or no voice.

The trouble with both big business and big labor is that they've lost sight of the value of the American worker and the need to involve him in the capitalist system. Business and labor leaders are both too caught up in their own power struggles.

The most graphic instance I know of this myopia is a conversation that took place some years ago between Walter Reuther and a Ford Motor Company executive. Reuther was a socialist; he wanted the Democratic Party to become a socialist labor party like the one in England. He was being shown through a new assembly plant with a lot of automated machines. The Ford executive said, "Walter, you're going to have a hard time collecting union dues from these machines," and Reuther replied, "You're going to have a harder time selling them cars." Neither of them thought of the obvious solution to their problem: give the workers the opportunity to invest in and reap the rewards from those machines.

What if the average American worker had two sources of income: one a paycheck for his labor and the other his share of the profits as a stockholder in the company? As the years went on and those profits grew in size and value, he could look forward to retirement just as someone now in top management looks forward to retirement, as a time to enjoy the returns of a sizable estate. The returns from a stock ownership plan are better than a pension program, which might or might not provide enough to keep up with inflation and which ends at the worker's death. A true stock ownership plan for employees builds their estates, which they can pass on to their heirs.

Some plants have already adopted stock ownership plans for their workers. Louis Kelso has designed them for company owners who want to retire and sell out to their employees. The key idea is to make workers also participating capitalists. Companies with profit sharing and stock ownership plans are showing a 3% higher per man-hour productivity than companies that pay just wages. And it takes only one-tenth of 1% increase in per man-hour productivity to add $1 billion to the gross national product.

To me this is the answer to socialism: to make sure that each worker has a piece of the action of capitalism. Abraham Lincoln signed the Homestead Act, which resulted in 53 million American families owning their own farms and homes. Now we need an "Industrial Homestead Act" so that workers can share in the capital gains of their labors.

Of all the statistics published by the federal government, perhaps the most closely watched by the greatest number of people is the unemployment rate. For most people, the word "unemployed" conjures up a picture of the head of a family laid off for several months without hope of having his job restored and worrying about how the mortgage can be paid and the family fed. But in truth less than 5% of those counted as unemployed fit this picture.

What the unemployment statisticians count, by sampling 47,000 households each month, is the number of people—men, women, and children, down to the age of 16—who didn't have a job the week they were called but said they had looked for a job in the past month. Included are teen-agers looking for their first jobs and married women whose husbands are working but who want to return to the work force after 10 or 20 years as housewives. Only half of the unemployed men over 20 are married.

The unemployment rate also contains all of those people who have quit one job to go to another or who are guaranteed a quick return to a job from which they were laid off. Even people who state to the statisticians that they are going to start work within 30 days are dutifully counted as unemployed. And technically they are. But whether or not the methodology for determining the unemployment rate is technically sound, it unquestionably produces a result different from the public's perception of the "unemployed."

What is full employment? Nobody really knows. There is obviously in any given week a certain percentage of the work force engaged in a normal turnover; going from job to job, from home to job, from school to job. They're obviously not unemployed in the sense of not having a job to go to. Whatever that percentage is currently—whether it's 2% or 3% or 4%—that's where we should start counting unemployment. If it's 3%, then a statistical rate of 4% would indicate that true unemploy-

ment was only 1%. And the government should say that to the people.

I also don't see how we can call some percentage the "unemployment rate" unless we include in it a subtraction figure for the number of jobs that are open. Many jobs go begging because there's no penalty for being unemployed. There was a time in this country when a person who couldn't get a job in his own line of work would take any job available. We were a mobile society; we moved to the jobs. Today welfare says we can't make people move to find jobs; we've got to bring the jobs to them.

All over the country there are job skills in short supply. How can we say that 500 welders are unemployed in Los Angeles if there are openings for 500 welders in Dallas? There should be a place in every city where a person can go to find out where in the United States his skills are needed.

There are also a lot of jobs available that some people now call "menial." Maybe we need to get back the Depression mentality, where there were no menial jobs. A job was a job, and anyone who got one felt lucky.

But above anything else, government should tell the people just what the unemployment problem is. If 35% of black teen-agers are unemployed and they're averaged in with the heads of household to make a composite unemployment rate of, say 8%, then it stands to reason that far less than 8% of heads of household are unemployed. Why aren't the statistics broken down into groups when they're published? It's almost meaningless to say that the composite rate went up or down in a given month. We need to know what happened to teen-agers, what happened to working wives, what happened to heads of household.

In California we started a work experience program for welfare recipients. We required that welfare recipients who were able to work and didn't have to care for small children, work 80 hours a month at a community service task as a condition of getting the welfare check. The welfare rights leaders screamed that this was slave labor. The Washington social reformers were fearful that we would be using welfare recipients to perform "menial" tasks that no one else would do. And we had to overcome the public misconception that welfare recipients were too lazy to work.

Here are a few actual examples of what happened. One man was considered unemployable because of his appearance and work attitude. After a short stint in the work experience program, an employment counselor was able to place him in a regular job repairing furniture in a furniture warehouse. He is now off welfare. Another man, 53 years old with a second grade education, hadn't worked for two years when the program started. He was assigned to the local school district as a custodial aide. After eight weeks he was hired permanently as a grounds keeper at $495 a month. A woman with some accounting skill was unable to get a job. She was assigned to the office of the County Auditor who, after watching her work for three weeks, hired her permanently as an account clerk.

These people, and they're typical of a great many on welfare today, weren't lazy at all. For whatever reasons, they had gotten out of the work habit; they were afraid to leave the security blanket of welfare and face the competitiveness of the working world. The work experience program gave them the opportunity to prove to others and to themselves that they weren't lazy, that they didn't deserve to be treated as "blanket cases" by the welfare system. They found out, as everyone does, that work is their best security.

Health

One of the ironies of history is that wars produce the greatest advances in medical care. World War II started a revolution in health care techniques that is still going on today. And while the medical revolution may have prolonged many lives, it has also caused public uncertainty about the quality and safety of its innovations. Contributing to this uncertainty has been the memory of the shortage and the inadequacy of medical facilities during World War II. There were never enough doctors on the battlefield; perhaps there never could be in such a war. But because so many doctors had enlisted or been drafted, they were also in short supply at home. Overworked doctors in understaffed and often obsolete facilities inevitably made mistakes, leading people to question whether a doctor not worth drafting was a good doctor at all. The "wonder drugs" of wartime research seemed to work miracles but were often not available.

This volatile mixture of progress and uncertainty has generated a continuing argument as to whether health care in the United States is good and sufficient. Particular attention in the past 15 years has been focused on the health needs of the poor and the role of government in filling those needs.

We must remember that concern for the health of the aged and the poor is not the invention of liberal social reformers. This country has always recognized the need for government to help provide health care to those who can't afford it. That need

has traditionally been met by a combination of public hospitals—county hospitals, principally—and the willingness of doctors to provide free care when it was needed. With all of the abuse that's being heaped on the medical profession today, everybody is ignoring the fact that, until Medicare and Medicaid came along, virtually every doctor had a list of patients for whom he never expected to get paid. Occasionally he might send them a small bill, to let them know that if things got better for them he would expect something for his efforts. But with most of them he didn't really expect payment.

Another fact conveniently ignored by the reformers is that most doctors charged their patients just as the government advocates today—on the basis of their individual ability to pay. Yet the care and attention were the same whether the patient could afford to pay a lot, a little, or nothing at all.

The federal government suddenly said that it would pay for all those patients the medical profession had been taking care of for nothing. As Bastiat * once said, "Public funds seemingly belong to no one, and the temptation to bestow them on someone is irresistible." So the doctors and hospitals started to bill the government for services they had once given away.

Harry Truman started the serious push toward socialized medicine in 1945, with a proposal for national health insurance. It took 15 years—until 1960—for the proponents of a federal health program to secure passage for a law providing federal medical payments for people over 65 who could prove need. In 1965 Medicare was enacted, providing federal medical payments to all Social Security recipients, regardless of need. At the same time the Medicaid program extended benefits to non-Social Security persons of all ages who could demonstrate that they were "medically needy." Currently several proposals for a comprehensive national health program are being discussed in Washington. If passed, such a program would

*Frédéric Bastiat, a nineteenth-century French economist.

constitute socialized medicine, since all doctors and medical facilities would be paid by, and would therefore in effect work for, the federal government.

The progress toward socialized medicine has been calculated and steady. When John Kennedy signed that federal medical assistance law in 1960, the congressman who had led the fight for its passage for several years stood on the steps of the White House and said, "At last we have our foot in the door, and this is only the beginning." That was long before I ever thought I'd be a governor. Now I've been one for eight years and am back in private life, and they're still at it.

Even then a better alternative was obvious to me. Granted that there were people who couldn't provide enough health insurance for themselves and their families. And granted that some of them, out of pride, wouldn't accept the charity of the doctors, and so stayed away and were not getting adequate health care. Some government help was necessary. But why should the government set up another bureaucracy to perform yet another task for which it was unqualified? The same result, at much less cost and much less danger to our democracy, could have been accomplished if the government had purchased insurance for those who couldn't afford it from private health insurers. The government could have set the standards; the insurance companies could have designed the policies to meet those standards, and the amount of the government insurance payment could have been calculated on the basis of federal income tax returns. The government could have paid all or a part of the insurance premiums on a sliding scale based on income and size of family.

There would be economic and social advantages to such a program. All of the administrative overhead would be absorbed by the private sector, which always spends less than government for administration. More importantly, the individuals being helped in this way would go to doctors as privately insured patients, and there would be nothing to indicate to a doctor or hospital that they were receiving government aid, that they were different from other privately insured patients.

Why is it that government is incapable of designing a program to help people without destroying their pride? The ubiquitous government medical card, like food stamps and other printed identifiers of government-supported charity, brands the carrier as "unfortunate" or "disadvantaged." As often as not, it is a cause as well as an indicator of dependence. Can it be that social reformers are afraid of pride because proud people won't do what the reformers want them to?

Socialized medicine has always been one of the key elements in programs of collectivization. Bismarck endorsed it to gain control of the German peoples, even though he personally hated socialism. "Health care for all" is an emotionally appealing idea. And once you socialize the doctors, you're well on the way to socializing the patients, who are all of us. So medicine is one of the vital striking points of collectivists.

The medical profession, as a profession, is very unpopular right now. Doubtless, despite the high ethics of the profession, there are a few doctors who'll grab a chance to make an easy buck. But there are a few people like that in any profession. We don't indict all clergymen because a few of them violate the cloth.

I think the feeling against the medical profession is mainly the result of propaganda and political rhetoric by the collectivists. Otherwise, how do you explain the results of last year's national poll on the adequacy of health care. Close to 90% of those polled were convinced that there was a national health crisis. But 90% also said that they didn't have any complaints with the medical care they received personally. They found it available, fair, and adequate. Through the propagandizing of socialized medicine proponents, people have come to feel that, while they personally are receiving adequate health care, no one else is. And with that feeling comes the humanitarian desire to help all those other people.

If those figures are correct, the so-called national health care problem probably involves less than 10% of our people. Common sense dictates that we find a solution for the 10%. What justification is there for forcing 100% of the people to participate in a government program in order to solve a problem affecting less than 10%? What justification, except the desire of the collectivists for more socialism and more control over all of our lives?

There is also a complaint that doctors in the United States are not evenly distributed and that many rural areas have no doctors at all. But how big is that problem? The last report I saw showed a nationwide total of 500,000 people living in 138 counties in which there was no resident physician. That means the problem affects one quarter of one percent of the population. And some of these areas are already finding doctors without Washington's help. Communities have subsidized the training of a medical student on the condition that he or she will practice in that community for a certain number of years. If the problem is acute, the federal government could help fund this kind of solution without making government employees of all the doctors.

People who feel that they have received improper medical treatment have always had access to civil courts for redress of their grievances. However, in recent years the number and size of malpractice awards have ballooned, and with them the cost of malpractice insurance. Malpractice insurance rates have climbed until doctors are being forced into early retirement or other occupations. The public, conditioned to distrust the medical profession, tends to blame the doctors, or at least not to feel sympathy for them.

No fair assessment of the malpractice insurance question can leave out the legal profession, some members of which used legal technicalities to drum up malpractice trade. Unquestionably the biggest health care crisis facing us today is the issue of malpractice. The costs of malpractice insurance contribute significantly to rising medical costs, but the threat of malpractice suits, with or without merit, costs even more. A doctor whose best judgment previously would have been to provide a patient the minimum treatment necessary to good health now orders every test and prescribes every treatment in the book to insure himself against a malpractice suit. He can't take a chance on his best judgment; the court is likely to think that's not good enough. The doctor has to build an exhaustive record that no one will be able to question.

I know one doctor whose malpractice insurance premiums are less than one-third the average for his fellow doctors in the same speciality. He's a relatively young surgeon, with a high-risk practice that would normally subject him to very high malpractice premiums. He has kept them low simply by his personal record keeping. He was one of a group of doctors who treated a patient who later filed a malpractice suit. His name was dropped from the suit when the plaintiff's lawyers saw how exhaustive his records were. But, after all, how much time should a doctor have to spend writing to protect himself from lawsuits?

It's disgraceful when a competent doctor is driven out of medical practice because he cannot afford to protect himself against malpractice suits. It's equally disgraceful when a doctor, who would otherwise be sensitive to the ability of his patient to pay, orders an expensive series of tests against his best professional judgment, because he feels he can't afford not to.

RIGHT: The Reagans. From left, Patty, Nancy, Ronald, Mike, Maureen, and Ronald. *"The whole duty of parents is to bring up their children with a sense of values."* BELOW: Ronald Regan in a variety of public moods. Reagan's *"personal and political philosophies are identical, and he is the same in private as he is in public."*

Opposite, TOP: Ronald Reagan with his wife Nancy as he announces his candidacy for the presidential nomination. *"Nancy made up her own mind that marriage was a career in itself, and she does darned well at it."* MIDDLE: A meeting of the California Youth Commission established by Reagan to advise the governor and the legislature on the problems affecting youth in the state. *"I would be as opposed to having my own philosophy imposed on these young people as I am at having liberal philosophy imposed on them."* BOTTOM: Reagan watches blind and near-blind children examine sculpture at a California Arts Commission travelling exhibition. *"Americans still have a great deal of generosity and compassion down deep inside. That concern for others is what's holding our society together."* ABOVE: The Reagans meet with President and Mrs. Luis Echeverria Alvarez of Mexico. BELOW: A controversial American leader holds a press conference in London. *"The self-sufficiency and material well-being of Americans are being diminished by government. We're following England down the road to intellectual and financial destruction."*

BELOW: Under Reagan's governorship the California National Guard was more than just a state militia. It sponsored, among other things, a youth tours program for residents of Hunter's Point, a low-income district in San Francisco. Here Reagan meets to discuss the program with representatives of the Urban League and the Guard.

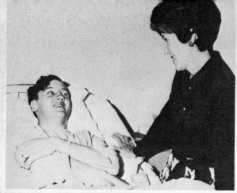

LEFT: Nancy Reagan cheers up wounded Viet Nam veterans at the Oak Knoll Naval Hospital, Oakland, California.

ABOVE: *"To complete the [welfare] reforms we needed changes in the state laws, and of course the [California] legislature just laughed at us."* To show the people the effects of the legislature's inaction, Reagan hung a poster in the main Capitol corridor and explained it to the press.
BELOW: *"The people were the real reason the [welfare] reforms worked [in California]. We took our case to the people and pretty soon the people let their legislators know they wanted action."* Reagan thanks Dell Yelverton and Carolyn Adamson of Whittier, California, who gathered 7,300 signatures demanding welfare reform. Right of Governor Reagan is Republican Senator George Deukmejian in whose district the women reside.

ABOVE: "The trouble with big business and big labor is that they've lost sight of the value of the American worker and the need to involve him in the capitalist system." Regan campaigns for governor among the workers of California. RIGHT: Reagan with Senator James Buckley of New York. "We must have leadership that will go over the heads of the bureaucrats, the Congress, the favor-seeking businessmen and union leadership: leadership that will speak directly to the people." BELOW: Governor Ronald Reagan of California meets Congressman Gerald Ford of Michigan in 1968.

Officially the protector of the public against dangerous drugs is the Food and Drug Administration (FDA), an arm of the federal Department of Health, Education, and Welfare.

I've heard drug experts say that they believe penicillin, if it were discovered today, would not be licensed by the FDA.

I think the FDA has gone overboard on procedures and paperwork, the symptoms of the bureaucratic disease. For example, just a few years ago one drug firm applied to license a new prescription drug and submitted some 70 pages of data to support that application. Last year, that same drug company submitted another application for another drug and had to send 73,000 pages of supporting documentation. In the last few years there has been a 60% reduction in the development of new medicines, and the delays in licensing caused by the FDA have added an estimated $200 million to the cost of the drugs we buy.

I'm not suggesting that the drug companies be turned loose to sell whatever they've found that they think might be helpful. But when you look at the record, we weren't in that much danger when it only took 70 pages to support an application for licensing.

There are also problems that no amount of time and documentation will reveal. Allergies are an example. We know that virtually every substance is an allergen to someone and that allergic reactions can run the gamut from a mild rash to sudden death. But does that mean that we should ban or withhold a valuable drug because a few individuals may be allergic to it? The logical answer is not to withhold life-saving drugs, but to find ways to protect the few individuals who might be allergic.

Years ago when I was making motion pictures, I smashed my thigh—broke it in six places. At the hospital my doctor—an orthopedic surgeon—decided that neither cast nor traction alone would be sufficient to hold the leg together. Instead of a cast he sheathed it with alternating layers of adhesive and sheepskin, embedding the straps for traction between the layers. It worked fine, except that I turned out to be allergic to sheepskin. By the time they figured that out, it was too late to take off the sheathing without permanently damaging the leg. For the first two weeks I was in the hospital I almost never opened my eyes, first because they were so swollen from the allergy, and second because I was so doped up with antihistamines I couldn't stay awake.

I recovered and went back to making pictures, and one of the first was a Western, shot on location in the Mojave Desert. The wardrobe people put me in a pair of old-fashioned sheepskin western pants. The first thing I knew, the pants were established in the scene, so I had to keep on wearing them, and I had a rash from my ankles to my hips. The temperature was about 100° in the shade, but the only thing I could do was put on long underwear under the pants because I was allergic to sheepskin.

But it wouldn't be right to ban sheepskin because I'm allergic to it.

On another subject—vitamins—I think the FDA has completely overstepped its authority. Only a couple of the vitamins have caused any adverse reactions in people, even when taken in enormous quantities. Here the FDA is not trying to protect us against dangerous drugs; it's trying to protect us from indulging in what it considers to be a worthless fad. Even if they're right in saying that extra vitamins are worthless to our health, preventing people from indulging in a harmless fad is none of the FDA's business.

What's more, I'm not sure they're right. I take a multiple vitamin pill every day, at the suggestion of a doctor. It's insurance against my not being able to eat balanced meals. And I've never felt better; I know that vitamin pill has been a help. The FDA isn't going to improve it. They're just going to regulate it enough to cause the price to rise.

One of the problems that a national health program is supposed to solve is catastrophic illness or injury, in which the requirements for treatment are more costly than most insurance policies cover. Reagan believes that this is a problem that government should help solve, but specifically and through the private sector, not as part of a comprehensive health care program.

Catastrophic illness can strike anyone; there's nothing a person can do about it in advance, and it can destroy a family financially. By definition it is any condition that requires constant and expensive medical procedures, such as hemodialysis or an iron lung. The costs in California per patient average $25,000 a year and may go as high as $100,000. We found about 10,000 cases in the state, out of a total population of 21,000,000.

We proposed to the state legislature a plan whereby the state would insure everyone, through private insurance companies, for the costs of catastrophic illness above those normally paid by personal and group insurance plans. It would have cost every working person $36 a year. But there was no interest among the people—so few were affected that the problem didn't get any press attention and the public didn't feel the need.

Yet here is one of the few problems that only government can accumulate the resources to solve. And this is a problem that must be solved, because when catastrophic illness strikes any but the most wealthy family, the family will almost certainly be wiped out, lose their home, and have to go on welfare to get the medical care they can't otherwise afford. It's ironic, but under the federal Medicaid program, people on welfare are provided free the medical care that working people can't afford.

Despite the need for specific solutions to specific problems, the proponents of a national health program continue to design grand solutions to problems that either don't exist or will be made worse by government intervention. Socialized medicine in England and Sweden provides graphic examples.

England has one doctor for every 1,200 people, roughly. We have one doctor for every 600. One of the reasons they're so short of doctors is that about one-third of their medical school graduates leave to practice in another country. They've built only three hospitals since 1948. We've built a dozen more than that in Los Angeles alone.

The social reformers use Sweden and England as examples of the wonders of socialized medicine. They don't bother to point out that in Sweden you can wait up to eight months to have your appendix removed, or that in England, the only women allowed to give birth in a hospital with a doctor in attendance are those having a first child or complications that could cause an emergency. All others must give birth at home with only a midwife in attendance.

A comparison of our system to those of England and Sweden should convince us to go in exactly the opposite direction from them.

I don't know any doctors who think they're infallible or that our medical care system can't be improved. But so much criticism of the medical profession is based on the determination of some social reformers to get the whole field of health care under the control of the government.

I wonder how many other professionals or craftsmen have thought about what will happen to them when this precedent of government control of a profession is established. There will be nothing to prevent the government from declaring plumbers essential to the national well-being, which of course they are, and nationalizing them. Plumbers would

**be unable to pursue their trade unless they were
government employees.**

In the face of rising medical costs, uncertainties about
the quality of health care, and the threat of socialized
medicine, many Americans are taking a more active
interest in maintaining their personal health, which is
perhaps the healthiest thing they can do.

**Not long ago I saw a newspaper account of a truck
driver who placed an ad offering his labor for one
full day a week to any farmer who had need of it.
He had grown up on a farm and didn't feel he was
getting the kind of exercise he needed driving a
truck. After fending off several skeptical inquiries,
he finally went to work for no pay for a farmer
who couldn't afford to hire any help. His rationale
was "Why should I pay money to go to a gym or
a health farm when I can do the healthiest kind
of work there is and help somebody out at the same
time?"**

Welfare

The essence of the welfare problem is that we're all torn between two perfectly reasonable attitudes: we want to help the person who's old or disabled or temporarily down and out, but we don't want to support the loafer who just doesn't want to work. Both get welfare, thanks to the misplaced benevolence of the federal welfare system. Our attitudes aren't wrong or inconsistent; it's the system that's out of kilter.

One of Ronald Reagan's most significant accomplishments as governor of California was welfare reform: a top to bottom shake-up of the welfare programs in his state. From a small, temporary relief program in the thirties, welfare had mushroomed until by 1970 it was straining state and local budgets all over the country, even though the federal government was paying more than half of the costs. In California alone, more than three billion dollars were being spent annually on more than two million welfare recipients—over 10% of the state's population—and the roles were increasing by 40,000 persons each month as new federal laws and regulations constantly loosened eligibility requirements.

Reagan's predecessors had studiously avoided the welfare issue: it was considered too hot to handle.

When I campaigned for governor, people kept telling me, "Don't mention welfare; that's political suicide." It was a big problem and growing worse, and

94

I felt that I had to talk about it. And I found, wherever I campaigned, the more working people there were in the audience, the more upset they were about welfare. They were closer to the problem and more aware of it. A guy comes out of his front door to go to work and sees the guy across the street just sitting there drawing welfare. He gets hot and bothered about that. And he gets more hot and bothered about when his elected leaders can't explain it to him, or when they give him some elaborate, legalistic reason dreamed up by the welfare bureaucrats to justify the expansion of their empire. All he knows is that he shouldn't have to pay for that guy's permanent vacation.

To reform welfare in California, Reagan faced the combined resistance of the federal and state welfare bureaucracies, the California Legislature, and the special interest groups who were profiting from the easy flow of welfare money. But he had the people on his side. Working through a small task force of public administration experts not tied to the welfare bureaucracy, Reagan initiated in early 1971 a reform program that not only stopped welfare growth but actually reduced the numbers of Californians on welfare by more than 400,000 in three years, saved the California taxpayers more than a billion dollars and, at the same time, raised the level of welfare payments to the poorest families—those with no workers and no other sources of income—by 30% or more above prereform levels.

The people were the real reason the reforms worked. Our program was reasonable and fair; it didn't deprive anyone of welfare who honestly needed it. But it did require people who could work to go to work, and it took off the rolls those for whom welfare was a bonus to an otherwise adequate income. To complete the reforms we needed changes in the state laws, and of course the legislature just laughed at us. So we took our case to the people, and pretty soon the people began to let their legislators know that they wanted action. The flood of telegrams, cards, and letters was so great that finally the speaker of the California Assembly came into my office with his hands up. He surrendered, and we got the new law we needed.

Other governors watched in amazement as California's welfare caseload and costs dropped while theirs continued to rise. One by one they sought Reagan's help, and by 1974 most of the states with the largest welfare problems had implemented some or all of Reagan's reforms.

Could the same thing be done to the federal program?

Certainly. Congress will bow to the will of the people, just as the California Legislature did. You don't have to convert Congress—save their souls—you just have to make them feel the heat. When they come home for a few weekends and find their constituents upset, and then they go back to Washington and compare notes, they'll change their political thinking.

But it will take more than a change in political thinking to solve the welfare problem. The welfare system produces the wrong result; it promotes greater dependence and insecurity in welfare recipients instead of providing opportunities for independence. It operates to increase, rather than decrease, the need for welfare, and it's not hard to figure out why.

I remember my first experience with it. I was still in school, during the Depression. My father had taken his lumps, like just about everyone else. In fact, I have to laugh whenever I read that someone doesn't think I understand the problems of the poor. We were damned poor. But because Roosevelt won in 1932 my father, who had always been a Democrat in a Republican stronghold, was able to get a government job. He was put in charge of the WPA (Work Projects Administration) in our area. There were two programs: WPA, which put

people to work, and direct relief, which was the forerunner of today's welfare. The people sent out to run direct relief were degreed social workers from the University of Chicago. It was the first we'd ever heard of professional welfare workers. In those days in a small town in Illinois, the unemployed were all men who had worked all their lives. They didn't enjoy welfare. They kept coming to my father and saying, "Jack, can't you get me onto one of your WPA jobs? I want to work." But my father couldn't place them because the social workers who were running direct relief didn't want to reduce their caseloads. They were afraid they wouldn't be able to justify their jobs, so they would invent all kinds of reasons why those men couldn't be made available for WPA work.

The need of those who manage and operate government welfare programs to justify themselves and their jobs has been one of the pressures for greater benefits and easier eligibility. The result has been that often people can do better financially on welfare than they can by working.

When welfare tempts a person to say, "I am better off not working than working," then we're destroying a human being. We may be feeding him, keeping him alive, but we've destroyed something very important in the human spirit.

On the other side of the welfare equation the taxpayers have lost patience and, even more significantly, the nation is rapidly losing its tradition of generosity.

One of the great tragedies in the whole welfare scandal, and it is a scandal, is that here in America have lived the most generous people the world has ever known. There's no country in history in which the people have been so willing to help each other or to help other countries in need. Now I don't think it's in the bloodstream of an American to be more charitable than someone from another country. Generosity has been a way of life here; an American accepted the responsibility to help his neighbor so that both of them could remain free, one from taxes and the other from the dole.

In other countries, countries belabored by generations of bureaucracy, people have grown up with the idea that there was somebody in government to take care of every problem. Now that's happening to us. More and more Americans are becoming accustomed to saying, when a problem comes up, "Well, that's government's responsibility." They forget that they pay for government, and that any problem left to government for solution costs them money and freedom.

I've never met a welfare recipient who thought down deep that he was a free citizen. The great majority would like nothing better than to be taking care of themselves. But they're all tarred by the same government brush. And the average worker, the guy who has always been the most charitably inclined; now his back stiffens when he sees someone on welfare. That isn't right. If we lose our generosity, we lose one of our most precious assets, one of the most important ways we have to protect our liberty.

The loss of personal concern for other is perhaps most visible in young people.

There are a great many young people who are compassionate for humanity. But they don't like people. They will bleed for a great cause, for humanity, but they don't have time for people. I think most of that comes from the classroom. They've been indoctrinated with the philosophy that government regulation and control are always the answer, and that the private economy is helpless without government management.

Government welfare is also an economic drain, which manifests itself in higher rates of inflation.

98

The fact that the federal government is spending more than it's taking in is complicated by the additional fact that we've declined in productivity. We now rank fourteenth in the world in annual increase in per man-hour productivity. Our inflation rate reflects both this decline and the federal deficit spending. But welfare also adds to inflation by spreading the means to produce.

The public, although dissatisfied with welfare, is not well-informed enough to know precisely why.

The people have been fed a steady diet of misinformation by nonproducing special interest groups ranging from the privileged few and their bureaucracies in the well-funded foundations to welfare rights and social work organizations. Our job is to get the real facts before the people so that they know that their distaste for government welfare is correct, and why it's correct.

One of the results of misinformation is the commonly held notion that welfare growth results from rising unemployment. Reagan's welfare task force in California compared unemployment rates and welfare caseload figures from 1955 to 1970. They found that during that 15-year period the unemployment rate went steadily down while the number of welfare cases went steadily up. Not only was unemployment not contributing to the growing welfare load, there was actually an inverse correlation between unemployment rates and welfare growth.

Who, then, is unemployed?

We know that the bulk of the unemployed are not heads of household desperately trying to support their families. There are some of those, and they are the most tragic cases of all in a recession. But most of the unemployed are teen-agers, and the reason they can't get jobs is, in part, the minimum wage laws. Every time we've raised the minimum wage, the unemployment rate among teen-agers has

99

jumped. Another thing that militates against the teen-ager getting work is all of our well-intentioned social reforms, which are supposed to protect young people, but which really just draw them into the government's grasp at an early age. Why should we be taking social security taxes from the pay of a teen-ager working part-time? Why, other than to feed government's greed? It certainly has nothing to do with the teen-ager's welfare.

A sound welfare system must encourage independence and preserve the dignity of those who need help; it must not destroy our tradition of generosity or drain our economy. Designing it and putting it into operation will take "... some great and imaginative thinking," and a drastic reduction in government involvement, since

... you generally don't get that kind of imaginative thinking from government.

Despite what they say, government social planners aren't interested in seeing a welfare recipient get on his feet and take care of himself. They'd rather he'd stay dependent on them, because he's their reason for existence.

Welfare reform must start from the assumption that everyone can contribute something productive to this society. Then the goal becomes to make as many people as possible independent of the need for welfare.

There is a division among people on welfare. First, there are those people who, because of age or disability, must depend on the rest of us permanently for help. I think we should do our utmost to provide them with more of the luxuries of life. And we should encourage their participation in areas where they can contribute their knowledge or time. An example is the foster grandparent program, in which elderly recipients get extra money for spending time with mentally retarded children. These people give love to children who need it badly, and who can't get it anywhere else. If that's not a worthwhile contribution to society, I don't know what is.

Then there are the other people on welfare, the ones who are temporarily unable to support themselves, because of lack of motivation or training or education. In a sound welfare system, any job should look like an improvement. And until they find paying jobs, there are public projects that can be done. The taxpayers have a right to say, "Here's a job that needs doing, and if we help you out with a welfare check, you can help us out by contributing your efforts to the good of the community."

But most importantly, no one should be sold short, as are millions in the present welfare system. We categorize people as aged, blind, disabled, or for some other reason unable to work, and count them out entirely as productive members of society. They become totally and permanently dependent on welfare, not because they need to be, but because our benevolent paternalistic government tells them they are.

Administering a welfare system that is aimed at making people self-reliant obviously cannot be left to government, especially not the federal government, which has a history of encouraging and sometimes forcing people to be dependent on it.

Government should set minimum standards to protect people, and government should also help in solving coordination problems, which is one of its legitimate functions. But the people and agencies that operate welfare must not have a vested interest in seeing how big they can make the program, as government always has.

One idea for administering a reformed welfare system is to turn welfare money over to profit-making welfare corporations owned and operated by welfare recipients. Anyone needing welfare would have to join one of the corporations, and in joining would receive one share of stock and the right to receive welfare as needed. No one eligible under present rules could be turned away. The government would pay each corporation the combined welfare benefits of its members. Since each member would have one share of stock, control of the corporation would always be vested in a numerical majority of its members.

The corporation would have two functions: to provide welfare when needed and to decrease the need for it. The corporation would pay welfare grants from government funds allocated to it; it would decrease the need for welfare through co-operative purchasing, short-term investment of funds, and job development. Properly managed, the value of the corporation and the monetary worth and job opportunities of its members would rise, while the influence of government and the need for welfare funds would decrease. Expert management assistance for the corporations could be provided by allowing income tax credits to experienced managers who volunteer and have their services accepted by the corporations. To protect against outside takeover, the volunteers would not be allowed to become members or officers of the corporations.

This "bottoms-up" approach to solving the welfare problems utilizes the strengths of capitalism and free-enterprise democracy, techniques that have never been applied to welfare, mainly because government social planners don't know much about capitalism. One of the contributing factors to the making of the present welfare "mess" has been the lack of reliance on traditional American approaches to problem-solving.

I wonder sometimes how we might have attacked this problem differently from the beginning. What if, in the dark days of the Depression when the welfare system was conceived, government had gone to the people instead of creating a federal welfare agency? What if the government had gone to the neighborhood churches and other charitable organizations and said, "How can we help you meet the needs of the poor? How can we coordinate your efforts to insure that no one is overlooked, and that only the people who need help get it? How can we help you get the people through this Depression and back on their feet?" If we had done that in the thirties, would there be twenty-five million people on welfare today, most of them hating to be on it as much as the taxpayers hate to pay for it? I don't think so.

Retirement Security

Social Security is in deep financial trouble, and the federal administrators are presenting Congress with only three solutions: raise taxes, lower benefits, or make Social Security a welfare program. Knowing predilections of Congress, we can almost guarantee that Social Security will become welfare, misusing the contributions of 80 million American workers. It doesn't have to happen, of course, but it will if we leave it to Congress and the bureaucrats.

The United States was founded by people who were seeking independence from strong central governments, and for 150 years that "Yankee independence" was the hallmark of the American spirit. But in the twentieth century, and particularly since the Depression of the thirties, more and more Americans have sought personal security, even at the cost of personal liberty. The federal government has responded with program after program promising more security to more people, borrowing heavily from the bureaucratic ideas and structures of those same strong central governments from which early Americans fled.

One of the principal protective programs of the federal government is Social Security, aimed at guaranteeing retirement and disability income to workers and their families. Social Security was begun 40 years ago, in response to the public outcry at the failure of private pension programs during the Depression.

Social Security started out to be simply an adjunct to normal savings, investments, and insurance. It was based on the traditional idea that families would feel and take responsibility for elders in their family groups. Social Security was intended to supplement family support and personal savings—to make sure that the elderly would have spending money of their own and wouldn't feel totally dependent.

The founders of Social Security called it a "floor of protection." A tiny fraction of each worker's pay—1% of the first $3,000 earned—matched by an equal amount from the employer, was to be put into a special insurance trust fund and paid out as a lifetime annuity to the worker when he retired.

Unfortunately, there was a basic flaw in the design of Social Security: Congress decided to create a government agency to collect the workers' contributions, pay out the retirement benefits, and manage the trust fund. What happened? The contributions became taxes; taxes that for the average worker are now twenty-five times higher than when the program started. Benefits fell victim to the "pork barrel" treatment of Congress, expanding in almost every election year since 1950. And the trust fund, unable to meet expanding benefits, was allowed to dwindle until now there isn't enough in it to pay a year's worth of benefits.

The sad fact is that if America's workers stopped paying their Social Security taxes today, Social Security payments to retired workers would stop within nine months, because the trust fund would be empty. That's not what I call a secure insurance program.

But even more appalling is the size of the future debt —the debt that Social Security is obligated to pay in coming years to people now retired or still working.

The government is presently committed to future Social Security payments of more than $4 trillion —and those are today's dollars, not adjusted for future inflation.

There's another way to look at the debt: a way used by economists and investment experts. It's called the "present value" actuarial deficit, and it means the amount of money you'd have to put into a savings program now in order to have enough in combined principal and interest to pay costs in the future. The Social Security Administration has calculated that amount to be at least $2.1 trillion, as of June 30, 1973. That's more than twice the sum of all the personal incomes of all the citizens of the United States for that year, and $800 billion more than the gross national product.

Just imagine, we could invest all of our incomes for two years in, say a mutual fund—if there were one that big—and still not have enough money to pay future social security benefits. That's how far out of balance the Social Security program has become.

More than 95% of the workers in the United States pay Social Security taxes, and those taxes amount to almost 12% of the average family's income. In 1975 a family with gross earnings of $14,000 paid $1,638 to Social Security, half of it coming from their paychecks and half from their employers.

But there are a privileged few who don't have to pay those taxes and don't have to worry about the effects of potential Social Security bankruptcy on their retirement incomes. The civilian employees of the federal government—some 3 million of them —have lobbied feverishly for 40 years to keep themselves out of Social Security. Now that it's in trouble they have nothing to lose. All these years they've been betting *our* money on a sure loser, at no risk to themselves.

106

What are the losses—losses that the managers of the program are avoiding? A year ago Martin Feldstein, a noted Harvard economist, calculated the effects of Social Security on wages, savings, interest rates, and the gross national product.

He found that Social Security has cut private savings, and therefore the ability of our people to invest in and reap the rewards of national growth, by 38%. That's more than one-third of our national savings and investment potential lost because of one government program.

He found that the lost savings are reflected in an annual reduction in the gross national product of $120 billion, a loss of almost $600 for every man, woman, and child in the nation.

He found that, if there were no Social Security, wages would be 15% higher and interest rates 28% lower. For an average family that would mean a $2,100 a year raise and a drop in their house mortgage interest rate from 8% to 6%.

The biggest losers are the middle and low income workers and their families. Their money makes up virtually all of that 38% loss in personal savings. When it started, Social Security took about $3 out of every $100 that the average family could save or invest. Today it takes $80. Thus what little money that family could be setting aside, perhaps to buy some bonds or a piece of land, is virtually all taken by Social Security taxes. And all the people get in return for their lost savings is a government promise that, if there's money left in the trust fund when they retire, they might get enough of a handout to scrape by on, that, if inflation doesn't get it first.

On top of everything else, Social Security is unfair in the way it taxes and distributes benefits. Working wives are taxed at the same rate as their husbands but usually receive no individual benefits at all when they retire. Wives who don't work at job taxed by Social Security aren't eligible to share in their husbands' benefits unless they stay married more than 20 years. And no worker under the age of 40 can expect to get back as much money when he retires as he has put into the program while working.

As inequitable and unstable a program as Social Security is, it has become the principal source of retirement security for millions of retired American workers. The problems of Social Security cannot be solved by eliminating the program.

The first premise of any plan for alleviating the troubles of Social Security must be to keep the promise to the people who have now based their future planning on the expectation of being cared for by Social Security.

Faced with proposals to raise Social Security taxes, lower retirement benefits, or turn Social Security into welfare by infusing it with general tax funds, Congress appears ready to choose the welfare option, which will be least offensive to the people in the short term. The upshot will be that a few years from now retired workers will have to go on welfare to get back the money they "contributed" to Social Security.

Congress is flirting with a massive betrayal of the trust of every American worker who has contributed his wages to what he has been led to believe is an insured retirement annuity. What's more, that betrayal of trust is as unnecessary as it is immoral. Social Security can be reformed by simply restoring government to its proper role as the protector of individual choice.

Here's one proposal, published last year, which demonstrates what I mean. The proposal starts by removing the monopoly over basic retirement funds now exercised by the Social Security Administration. Social Security taxes would be eliminated, and both the employees' and the employers' shares added to the workers' wage. Each worker would then choose between investing in a government-insured private pension plan or a new series of U.S. Retirement Bonds with annuity payoff. The annual investment for each worker would be 10% of earned incomes or $2,500, whichever is less.

The bonds would increase in value every year by an amount that, in any one year, would at least keep up with the cost of living and, over a period of many years, would do considerably better. The bonds would have a lifetime annuity value at retirement, and also provide annuities to survivors in event of the worker's death, or to the worker and his family in case of disability.

The bonds would also be convertible, in any amount and at any time, into private pension funds at the option of the worker. Thus, the government and private pension plans would compete to see which could provide the best return, and the advantages of the competition would accrue to the worker.

Workers currently paying into Social Security would receive the accumulated value of their past contributions in bonds. Retired workers would continue to receive their Social Security pensions, but the amounts of the pension would grow each year at the same rate as the bond interest rate which, as I've said, would be at least as great as the growth in the cost of living.

In summary, each worker would be guaranteed as much retirement income as he had been led to expect from the present Social Security program, and without the possibility of Congress making him a welfare case or squandering his investments until there was nothing left to pay him. He could choose to invest in the private pension market, with potentially higher returns from private investments. General taxes would be used to retire the bonds, thus eliminating the unfair Social Security tax burden and putting more money for savings or investments into the hands of low and middle income workers and their families. The traditional American principles of preventing monopoly and expanding individual choice would slowly but surely work the program out of its present debt.

Every member of Congress has a copy of this proposal. Why haven't they given it serious consideration?

The answer to Reagan's question reveals the severe limitation of congressional thinking. Following the "conventional wisdom" of centralized government regulation and control urged on it by the bureaucracy of the Social Security Administration, Congress has been unwilling to consider seriously proposals to increase individual choice, such as Reagan has described.

One of these days they're going to reap the harvest of ill will of younger workers who come into Social Security and discover that Congress is robbing them blind. There is a real danger that when that happens all workers, active and retired, will suffer. We must restructure the Social Security system before it collapses.

Crime and Justice

There is no single reason why the crime rate keeps rising in America. But up near the top of the list must be the sad fact that so much of our criminal justice system has become a technical game between lawyers, without regard for guilt or innocence.

The rise in crime rate in the past 20 years, as reflected in ever more elaborate and frightening crime statistics, has become a major concern to most Americans. Although some of the concern may be the product of better information collection and more graphic reporting, it is undoubtedly true that Americans are now in greater danger of being victims of violent crimes, especially in the cities, than they have been at any time in recent history. Nor does the crime wave reflect economic conditions; in 15 years of steady prosperity, crime rates steadily rose. In the past five years of fluctuating recession and prosperity, crime rates have continued to rise.

It's obvious that prosperity doesn't decrease crime, just as it's obvious that deprivation and want don't necessarily increase crime. It's my recollection that crime rates were at their lowest during the Depression of the thirties, when great numbers of people were destitute. Today's criminals, for the most part, are not desperate people seeking bread for their families. Crime is the way they've chosen to live.

Assuming that, in a complex society, choice is partially free and partially not, it is necessary to explore the determinants of choice to discover root causes of crime. The emotion-producing catch phrase, "crime in the streets," points to the obvious concentration of crime in urban areas.

A friend of mine—an educator—recently spoke to a father-and-son banquet. Thinking about the crime problem in the cities, he asked the fathers present to raise their hands if they had grown up in homes in which the front door was left unlocked at night. Every father raised his hand. Then my friend asked how many of the sons had had the same experience, and not one raised his hand. Suddenly, when he told me this, I realized that I couldn't remember as a kid whether my family ever had a door key. I don't recall ever seeing a key in our house.

But of course I grew up in a small town. When I started growing up and when the fathers at the banquet started growing up, 70% to 75% of Americans lived in small towns or on farms. Today, 70% to 75% of us live in cities. In the city victims are conveniently gathered together, and a criminal can get lost in the crowds. In a small town or in the country he is likely to be recognized, because everyone knows everyone else. George Washington warned us that "the violence of the cities is to be feared," and went on to point out that there had been a history of crime whenever people had lived jammed together in a city.

While it is true that more people are now living in urban areas, it is also true that in the past 15 years the population density of urban areas has decreased—people are spreading out into the suburbs, gaining more area per person for themselves and leaving behind more area per person for those who remain in the central cities. Still the crime rate rises.

Another factor in the current crime situation is the mood of violent revolution, the idea that this society must be pulled down. I believe a large part of that mood is not accidental, not a spontaneous uprising at all. I believe it has been contrived as part of the world ideological struggle between totalitarianism and democracy. Nothing sets the stage for a dictator better than chaos, which is exactly what the revolutionaries are trying to create. No solutions, just bring down the society to make way for a new order, which is totally undefined.

How much crime is the result of this revolutionary mood I don't know, but the crimes connected with it are the most terrifying imaginable because they have no apparent motive related to the victim. The Zebra killings in San Francisco, for example, were random murders of complete strangers for no reason other than to kill and, I suppose, to horrify the populace. These people killed simply because that's what their organization was set up to do.

But if I had to choose the most important factor in the rising crime rate, I'd have to say it is the theory and operation of the criminal justice system. For 40 years the system has been dominated by people who believe that social injustice is the primary cause of criminal action. Taking this as an article of faith, and with the best of intentions, criminal justice theorists have developed program after program to rehabilitate, rather than incarcerate, criminals. Particularly with young criminals, children who commit crimes, there has been a systematic attempt to rehabilitate them through parole or probation rather than prison, head them off from a life of crime by assigning them for guidance to probation officers, the social workers of the criminal justice system.

These programs have failed, just as the social service programs in welfare have failed, and for the same reason. A paternalistic government allows no room for the individual to change and develop

113

himself—the government insists on doing it for him.

California has had a heartbreaking experience with criminal rehabilitation. When I was governor, we invested heavily in probation programs. We felt, as everyone feels, that throwing youngsters into prison was like sending them to a school for crime. So the state subsidized the counties' hiring of probation agents. Everyone seemed very happy with the program; the counties were delighted to get the money; the probation officers were overjoyed to get the work and, I'm afraid, the juvenile delinquents were just as overjoyed at the chance to develop their criminal skills outside of prison.

Pretty soon we found that no one was going to jail, and that the kid on the road to being a full-fledged criminal was recruiting others by showing them how, even if he were caught, he could be back out on the street in 24 hours, even back in school. The problem was compounded by the gamesmanship of attorneys in finding technical points to free even those criminals who would have gone to jail under our programs. And the courts went along with the game.

Early in our administration we were able to get passed a law that automatically added 5 to 15 years to the sentence of anyone who carried a gun during the commission of a crime. It was a tough but necessary law; even if the criminal didn't take the gun out of his pocket, he got the extra 5 to 15 years. In the first year after enactment, armed robberies decreased by 31%. But even before the year was over, the armed robbery rate had bottomed out and started to rise. In the second year it climbed back to what it had been before the law was passed. We couldn't figure it out, until we analyzed the court actions. The law had included a minor clause allowing the judges some flexibility —that's the fashion in laws these days—to waive the extra sentence under "exceptional circumstances." It had taken less than a year for everybody, including the judges, to find that anyone carrying a gun was an "exceptional circumstance" case, not subject to the extra penalty. When we tried to take the "exceptional circumstance" clause out of the law, the state legislature, in its infinite wisdom, buried the bill in a typical blizzard of inaction, letting it die in committee. So much for the protection of our citizens.

To me, the only workable gun control law is one that automatically sends a person to prison, for a long time, for committing a crime with a gun. The same people who pushed social reform ideas into the criminal justice system now want to take guns away from everyone. Well, God help us if a burglar prowling the street at night has a government guarantee that there is no gun in any home he may choose to enter.

When the gun control laws were first being proposed, I received a very interesting letter from a professional burglar in prison. He said, "Let me tell you from experience that the one thing we fear more than anything else in plying our trade is that we may have picked a home where the homeowner has a loaded gun in the bedside drawer. That's one thing we can't guard against. You tell us that there are no guns in the hands of the victims, and you've given us a winning ticket." As I learned, professional burglars seldom carry guns themselves, and would be overjoyed if no one else did either.

Proponents of government confiscation of all guns seem also to be among the most vocal advocates of the abolition of capital punishment. The death penalty, not imposed in the United States since 1967, was outlawed by the U.S. Supreme Court in 1972 as "cruel and unusual punishment," on the basis that its administration by the states was "arbitrary and capricious." Since 1972 many states, through legislation or initiative, have restored the death penalty for specific crimes, hoping thus to avoid the "arbitrary and capricious" judgment of the Supreme Court.

In California, only a few months after the Supreme Court decision, the people voted overwhelmingly to restore the death penalty. But the legislature dragged its feet for two years before it finally passed specific legislation to implement the people's decision.

Now the opponents of capital punishment in California and in the other states where it has been restored are asking why the rates of murder and other capital crimes hasn't declined. In my opinion it's because there hasn't yet been an execution. Just putting the death penalty back into the law books, after almost a decade of no executions, is not going to be a deterrent. But the first few times an execution makes the front page of the newspapers will make the difference. If that sounds cruel, think about some of the crimes committed in the last nine years—the Tate-La Bianca slayings, for example—for which the death penalty couldn't be imposed.

I believe that capital punishment is a deterrent to the most violent crimes, that it is a measure of self-defense for society to make certain that people who commit the most heinous crimes will not be able to repeat them.

In recent years there has been a growing tendency to look for and find crime throughout the fabric of our society. Widespread "victimless" crimes, such as tax and welfare fraud, embezzlement of company and bank funds, gross misuse of pension funds by union officials and, of course, Watergate: all seem to lend credence to the accusations of cynics that we are a criminal society in our institutions and in our selves.

I have read that the annual cost to business of employee pilferage and customer shoplifting is about

$4 billion. I wonder if that $4 billion isn't, in large part, the cost of impersonality. Not that pilferers and shoplifters aren't criminals—they certainly are —but that they don't feel anyone's being hurt by their crimes. The large corporation employee who fudges his expense account a little usually doesn't think of himself as dishonest. He may well be the same person who'd walk a mile to return excess change to a local storekeeper. But with the expense account, who loses? As far as he can see, only a large and impersonal corporation that can easily afford it. That's how he rationalizes his crime.

The same is true of fudging on taxes, but here we begin to see the pressures that lead the average citizen to cheat, and that make the rationalization that no one loses tempting, and eventually even necessary. Economists years ago pointed out that a society would bear its government taking up to 20% of personal earnings in taxes. Above 20%, some people would begin to evade paying full taxes. Above 25% there would be widespread resentment and cheating. And above one-third, the disrespect for government would eventually become disrespect for other people, followed by wholesale crime and the collapse of the society.

At our present level of taxation and government control, otherwise honest people begin to feel that they're being had. When government stops respecting the rights of the individual, the individual stops respecting government. And if that situation continues long enough, individuals also stop respecting each other's rights. That's what is happening to us.

Americans have always expected their judges to be fair and impartial, to balance objectively the requirements for an orderly society against the rights of the individual, whether that individual be the offended or the offender. These expectations have been based on the supposedly nonpolitical nature of the judiciary: judges are theoretically appointed for their legal expertise and judicial fairness.

But as government has grown more and more powerful, people have come to realize that judges are as politically motivated as legislators and as philosophically biased as professors, perhaps because so many of them have previously been one or the other.

The manner of appointing judges automatically causes them to reflect the economic and political philosophy of the government. For 40 years that philosophy has been predominantly liberal, predominantly one of advocacy of government imposed social reform. It's no wonder so many court decisions fall on the side of government control.

In the early days of the New Deal, Franklin Roosevelt ran head on into the U.S. Supreme Court, which began to find that some of his schemes were unconstitutional violations of personal liberties. He tried to get Congressional approval to "pack" the court, to add enough more members to it—members whom he could appoint—so that he could control it. He called the justices "nine old men living in the past." Congress refused to go along with him, thank heaven.

At the time I was a "New Dealer," and it's only in hindsight that I have been able to see what a blatant and inexcusable power play Roosevelt attempted. We still feel its effects, both because the very attempt helped politicize the courts even more than they had been, and because Roosevelt and his successors—most of them devout centralists— "packed" the courts over the years just as effectively as if Congress had approved Roosevelt's plan: by appointing one-sided judges to every court vacancy. We are now forced to live with 40 years of bench-warmed social reform.

Land Use and the Environment

The Fifth Amendment to the Constitution states: "No person shall . . . be deprived of life, liberty, or property, without due process of law; nor shall private property be taken for public use, without just compensation."

A person's property is entitled to the same protection as his life and liberty, with one exception. The government can take his property for a valid public use, but only if it pays him a fair price.

There may be room to argue over the definition of a valid public purpose, but certainly there can be no argument about compensation. If the government takes someone's land, it must pay him for it. The principle is that the government action cannot reduce the value of a person's property any more than it can take his life or restrict his freedom, unless he has committed a crime.

Nor does the Constitution distinguish between different kinds of property. It doesn't say a person has one kind of right to the money in his pocket and another kind of right to his home. In fact the Supreme Court said, in 1972, that "the right to enjoy property without unlawful deprivation . . . is in truth a personal right, whether the property in question is a welfare check, a home, or a savings account."

The United States has an unbroken tradition of private ownership of land predating its existence as a nation. The tradition itself is rare enough in the history of the world; the embodiment of that tradition in law is perhaps unique.

Before the United States there had been almost no opportunities for ordinary citizens to own land. Land belonged to the rulers to dole out to their friends. The Spanish land grants in the southwestern United States were gifts from the King of Spain. The Homestead Act, signed by Abraham Lincoln in 1862, was the first law that allowed an ordinary citizen freely to claim, work, and own the land with the protection of the federal government.

Under the Homestead Act more than a million families received title to 248 million acres, more than one-eighth of the nation's land.

Critics of our private land ownership system say that the land is in the hands of a few land grabbers. They ignore the fact that 40% of the land is still owned by government, yet 53 million families, containing 140 million people, now own their own homes. There is no major industry in the world in which ownership is so widely dispersed.

The term "land use planning" has come into vogue in the last few years, particularly in relation to protection of the environment and development of natural resources.

"Land use planning" is bureaucratic jargon devised by government planners to disguise their assaults on the constitutional right to property. "Land use planning" really means control of private lands. It means a person can continue to hold the deed to his property only if he uses it precisely as the government tell him to. "Land use planning" is a modernized version of Mussolini-style fascism,

120

which was so much admired by the New Deal social reformers before World War II.

Attempts by the government to control private lands aren't new. Cities and counties have long had the power to zone land uses. But that isn't good enough for the federal planners. They want to move the zoning power to Washington, D.C. and have one huge master zoning plan for the entire nation. The first step is to get Congress to pass the National Land Use Planning Act, which will force the states to initiate statewide management of zoning authorities. The next step will be to take management away from the states and entrench it in a new Washington bureaucracy.

Fortunately, Congress has successfully defended the Constitution and turned down the National Land Use Planning Act for the past two years. The planners will keep trying, however. They operate from within the security of the federal bureaucracy, and they can afford to keep coming back and coming back until they wear Congress down.

As an example of what the National Land Use Planning Act will mean to farmers and homeowners, here is what Congressman Morris Udall, one of the authors, said recently about the constitutional requirement for compensation: "In some cases, the local or state government may have to condemn and purchase property, but compensation should be required only where the regulation of use effectively denies an owner any economic return."

What Udall is advocating is that government be able to keep a farmer from growing anything but one beanstalk on his property, without having to pay him for his loss. This certainly is a cheap replacement for the farm subsidy program. If you think my example sounds farfetched, consider that there have already been cases in which people have been deprived by state and local governments of as much as 90% of the value of their property without any compensation. And that's without a national land use act.

It seems that government planners sometimes find it inconvenient to recognize personal rights to property, particularly if that property is the land they want to regulate. They prefer to confiscate the land, and if a person's home and livelihood are on it, well, that's unfortunate. That's his "contribution" to the "public good."

The reason the planners want to control our land is that they're both reformers and elitists. Like all reformers, they think they know what's best for us. Like all elitists, they are willing to sacrifice our rights to prove it."

One of the reasons usually given for the need for more government control of land use is to prevent land speculators from reaping windfall profits in land development.

How many speculators are there? I'll bet that for every speculator who makes a windfall profit there are a dozen who either go broke or never intended to speculate. For instance, am I a speculator? Some years ago I bought a ranch northwest of Los Angeles. People didn't even know about that part of the country and certainly weren't interested in living there. I didn't know it was there or how scenic it was until I started looking for a ranch. I bought it because I wanted to raise horses and because it was inexpensive enough that I could afford it.

I'd had the ranch 15 years when the state put in a freeway three and a half miles away. My ranch suddenly became real estate, which I couldn't afford to raise horses on. Property taxes, which had been $800 a year when I bought it, went up to $23,000 a year. I obviously sold it at a substantial profit, but not because I'd bought it to develop it into a subdivision. I had wanted to spend the rest of my life there and hand it on to my children.

I reinvested the profit in a ranch farther away, in hopes that civilization won't catch up with that

122

one before I'm too old to get any pleasure out of it.

The recent advocacy by planners and environmentalists of restricting or doing away with private land ownership has met with surprisingly little organized opposition. Two-thirds of our citizens own or are buying their homes. Why is it that a direct challenge to private land ownership seems to bother the public so little?

Perhaps part of the reason is that private ownership is already being done away with. The amount of privately owned land has not decreased in the past 15 years, but the right of property owners to use their land as they wish has certainly been diminished. Federal and state regulations, often requiring long and unpredictable public hearings, have been superimposed on local zoning. The result has been a virtual freeze on development in many areas with critical housing shortages, and uncertainty about present and future property values.

The erosion of real property rights reflects the central conflict of American democracy: the conflict between the concepts of individual liberty and the greatest good for the greatest number. In recent years those who favor the greatest good for the greatest number have had the better of it in the public media. Some of the more fervid proponents of the collective good have even tried to redefine individual liberty as the freedom to do what government commands.

I know there is evidence that we Americans may be changing from an independence-seeking people to a security-seeking people. If so, rigid national control of private land will become a reality. And other forms of personal property will follow the land. The automobile is already heavily regulated from Washington D.C.

On the other hand, there is a growing body of evidence that people in the states that have tried

123

centralized land use control don't like it. I believe there is a sticking point at which security has too thick a coating of regulation to be swallowed. And perhaps our own lack of diligence in telling the people what happens when individual liberty is sacrificed to the greatest good for the greatest number, has contributed to the indifference that meets threats to private ownership of property. If so, it's time for a correction.

Proponents of centralized land use control justify it on two grounds: preservation of the land for the people and protection of the land from the people. These two aims often conflict or overlap confusingly, as for example, in the demand for more parks that are accessible to fewer people. Traditionally local zoning boards have been the arbiters of public choice and demand.

I endorse local zoning for the protection of the property owner. I believe it is a proper local government function to assure that what one person does with his property does not harm another person. But even local zoning boards are subject to the same kind of pressure from special interests that is the bane of bigger governments.

One of our largest cities—Houston, Texas— doesn't even have local zoning. Yet its patterns of residential, commercial, and industrial development are not noticeably different from zoned cities and its property values have held up better than those in many elaborately planned cities. It doesn't have dairy farms or packing plants right next to housing developments. The free market and the covenants of freely organized neighborhood organizations have accomplished what everyone else has thought could only be done by government.

In several significant actions in the past few years, states have usurped local zoning authority to meet state-wide preservation and protection goals.

Let's take the establishment of the California Coastal Commission, in 1972, by a popular vote of the people, to control all development along the ocean. The voters were convinced that the coastline was rapidly being turned into private homes and resorts and that in a few years no one would be able to go to the beach.

The argument was made that there were only so many miles of coastline, and when it was all in private hands, there would be no more forever because it could never be reclaimed. At that time government owned 40% of the coastline and was not selling it off. But even if the coastline had been "disappearing" into private hands, as charged, there was no need for a state commission to control use of the entire coastline. The proponents of the Coastal Commission exhorted the people to "Save Our Beaches." That was never the real issue. The issue was government control of the coast.

Some people want to live on the ocean. Most people don't; they just want to be able to go to the beach once in a while. The people who want to live on the ocean should be able to buy a piece of the coastline and build on it. The people who want to go to the beach now and then should be able to buy, through the collective power of government, enough beachfront property to ensure that there will be beaches to go to. And that was exactly the situation before the Coastal Commission was created. The Commission hasn't created new public beaches but it has prevented many people from building private homes on what had been private land. The Commission has diminished the freedom of some of the people without adding one iota to the freedom of all the people.

One Saturday afternoon, during the campaign to decide whether or not there should be a Coastal Commission, I took a helicopter ride from Los Angeles to San Diego. Half of the people in California live in that area. It was the hottest Saturday of the summer, a record-breaking 102°. We passed several state beaches, some crowded and some virtually empty. They had the same facilities, and in some cases the crowded beach and the empty beach were within a quarter-mile of each other. Obviously many beach-goers prefer to be crowded together. Buying more beaches that people won't go to because they prefer to be crowded together on one beach is ridiculous waste of our natural resources and our taxes.

The California Coastal Commission is an example of a nationwide trend toward increased government regulation of private land use instead of government purchase of land that needs to be preserved. Although the Constitution requires just compensation as a condition of government land control, government planners feel that the public is unwilling to pay the taxes necessary to provide compensation. But, as Reagan points out, government control through regulation is not the only alternative to vast and immediate expenditures of tax monies for land purchase.

We can't look ahead 50 years, or even 20 years, and say with any certainty what our requirements are going to be for agricultural land, or recreational land, or even land for housing. And even if our guesses as to "how much" could be made more reliable, we couldn't solve the question of "where" to anyone's satisfaction.

One solution of the inherent unpredictability of future land needs is the use of government bonds to purchase land. A state government could offer to buy a farm, for instance, for bonds instead of cash, with the stipulation that the seller remain on the land and keep it in agricultural use until the bonds mature. In the interim, the seller would receive both the agricultural income from the property and the annual interest on the bonds. The effect of the transaction would be a government guarantee to the people that the land would be preserved as a farm, without the government having to lay out immediate cash to purchase it. If, in 10 or 20 years when the bonds mature, there is no longer any need to preserve publicly the land as a farm, the government could sell it on the open market. The final, and the most important, advantage to the use of bonds is that they require a vote of the electorate, and thus put into the hands of the voters the decisions about how much should be spent to preserve what kinds of land.

The second major problem of land use is environmental pollution. Protection of the environment against human despoliation has been a major public concern for the past 15 years, and control of pollution is cited as one of the primary justifications for a national land use act.

This is another subject that has been overdramatized by the use of selective statistics. The total amount of air and water pollution in a given area is most closely related to the number of people who live in that area. The environmental lobby says our urban areas are dangerously overcrowded because "70% of our people live on 2% of the land." That sounds shocking, but simple arithmetic shows up the statistical exaggeration. Seventy percent of the population is 140 million people. Two percent of the land is 40 million acres. That's one acre of land for every family in our most crowded urban areas. Is that overcrowding? Moreover, throughout the United States population densities in major urban areas have been falling steadily for more than 10 years. So have pollution levels. And that improvement has been accomplished without the benefit of a national land use act.

We still have too much air and water pollution, and we still need to work to reduce it. But we also need to put the problem of pollution into an historical as well as scientific perspective. It's not as frightening to hear some overzealous environmentalist say that air pollution is rapidly destroying civilization when we realize that people have lived in much dirtier air throughout history.

We know that the ancient Greeks, who were considered highly civilized, heated and cooked with a fire in the middle of a stone floor under a hole in the ceiling. They lived in fumes that must have been a thousand times worse than our worst air pollution.

We know that Cicero wrote of what a great relief it was to get into the open country and away from the terrible gases in Rome.

We know that Martha Washington wrote letters to friends, when the Capitol was in Philadelphia, complaining that everyone there had eye infections from the noxious fumes.

Smog is not the only air pollutant. Is smog from automobiles more dangerous, in a city like New York, than the effluvium of millions of tons of horse manure dropped in the streets and run over by carriages and wagons? Or more dangerous than the soft coal smoke that belched out of every chimney, from early fall to late spring, when I was a boy? In the thirties and forties all of the photographs and paintings of factories showed smoking chimneys to prove that the factories were operatin. A smokeless chimney was a sign of economic distress.

We still don't know enough about smog to control it intelligently. The catalytic converter and the earlier smog-control devices were installed under government pressure and without full knowledge of their effects. In California we required a device on every car that would reduce hydrocarbon emissions by 70%. Then we found out by reducing hydrocarbons we increased nitrates of oxygen, which turn the air brown. Last year Germany conducted an experiment to determine the effects of leaded and unleaded gasoline. They pumped leaded exhaust fumes into one greenhouse and unleaded fumes into another. Plants in both greenhouses were damaged, but when the exhaust fumes were turned off, the plants recovered faster in the greenhouse that had been pumped full of leaded fumes. What's more, not a trace of lead was found in the new vegetation after recovery.

Air pollution problems differ significantly with changes in the geography and climate. Los Angeles is a basin surrounded on three sides by mountains and on the fourth by the ocean. Any onshore breeze blows the pollutants against the mountains. Sunlight creates a temperature inversion that holds the pollutants down so they can't get over the mountains. Result: smog. But should there be a National Clean Air Act that requires Montana to take the same antipollution steps as Los Angeles, even though Montana has no comparable problem?

Water pollution also has local uniqueness, which make a uniform national solution ridiculous. Water carries virtually everything, and it's impossible to find a stream of "pure" water in nature. The question about any stream is whether its impurities are unhealthy or unpleasant.

When I was a boy, I was a lifeguard on a river beach on the Rock River in Illinois. It's one of the most beautiful rivers in the country, and it was naturally a popular recreation spot. In those days everyone understood that running water, with sunlight on it, purifies itself within several miles of where it becomes polluted. The next city, 35 miles upstream from us, dumped its raw sewage into the river. By the time the water reached us, it was clean. There were always crowds swimming during the summer, but no one got sick, and the water was pleasant. I was a lifeguard there seven years and never got sick.

Over the years the Rock River became so polluted that now no one swims in it in the park where I used to work. The cities grew larger and closer together and they continued to dump sewage into the river until nature couldn't handle it anymore. Recently they've started to clean it up; they've stopped dumping sewage and industrial wastes, and in a few years it will be back to normal. We made a mistake and we're correcting it.

But the water will never be "pure" water; it will always contain harmless amounts of many chemicals leeched from the soil or dumped in small quantities upstream. In contrast, the proposed clean water bill under consideration in Washington D.C. would require that everyone put back into rivers like Rock River 100% pure water. Not only is such a proposal scientifically silly, but implementing it would probably bankrupt the country.

For 15 years environmentalists have attacked the automobile as the chief air polluter in our nation. More recently a concerted effort has been undertaken to replace automobiles with mass rapid transit systems in major cities.

The automobile on the freeway is the greatest mass rapid transit system we've ever developed. There are people for whom other systems should be improved: those too old or too young to drive and those who can't or don't want to pay the cost of maintaining an automobile in a congested city. And unquestionably we've got to make the automobile cleaner and more efficient. I don't think the eventual answer is to hang more devices on it, which cost more money and cause it to run less efficiently. We've got to make it burn the fuel better.

Two of the best mass transit systems in the world are in New York and Chicago. And they're two of the worst cities for traffic problems and pollution. I'm a corneal lens wearer, and I have to take my lenses out to walk even a few blocks in New York, because the grit that gets between the lenses and my eyes is unbearable.

But the automobile gave man one of the last great freedoms that he'd never had before: the freedom of individual mobility. For the first time he did not have to depend on someone else's timetable and choice of route. Looked at historically, it is great freedom for man to be able to choose his time of departure, his route, where and when he is going to stop, whether he is going to make side trips. For all the abuse now being heaped on the automobile, there's nothing better on the horizon. When something better does come along, it will have to be better because it extends man's liberty.

Liberty and property have always been connected in the minds of Americans. The U.S. Supreme Court reaffirmed in 1972 that: "A fundamental interdependence exists between the personal right to liberty and the personal right to property. Neither could have meaning without the other."

Politics and Public Morality

I've always believed that the founding fathers never envisioned the government being run by professional politicians. I've always thought that they envisioned men like themselves, just good citizens, who would be willing to make a personal sacrifice and serve temporarily in government. The idea of a clique of profession politicians devoting all their energies to getting reelected was foreign to the thinking of Jefferson, Washington, and Hamilton.

Professional politicians like to talk about the value of experience in government. Nuts! The only experience you gain in politics is how to be political. We need leaders who know how to be leaders, people who know what it's like to be a private citizen burdened by a greedy government, people who will work honestly and openly to keep government from becoming any more of a burden than it has to be. That doesn't take government experience. That just takes common sense.

There's an old legend about the politician who looks out his window and sees his constituents marching by. "There go my people," he says. "I must hasten to find out where they're going so I can get in front and lead them."

We have an even worse leadership problem. Our leaders refuse to level with us about national problems. In 1967 there were antiwar riots in 127 cities and on probably as many campuses. One hundred thousand people marched on the Pentagon. Not until last year was it reported by a newspaper columnist that in that terrible year Lyndon Johnson had called the leaders of Congress to the White House and presented them with documented proof that the international communists were one of the forces behind the riots. Gerald Ford, then the minority leader of the House of Representatives, asked why the American people were not being told. Ramsey Clark, then the Attorney General, reportedly said that the American people couldn't be told because "it would start another wave of McCarthyism."

Americans have always had a healthy suspicion of politics and politicians. In the past 10 years suspicion appears to have hardened into hostility, hostility focused on Watergate. Is the hostility also healthy? Has Watergate helped or hurt the nation?

I think Watergate has hurt us. A recent poll of high school seniors revealed that 81% of them believe that people elected to public office are without honor and integrity. Four years ago only 21% were so disillusioned. A large part of this extreme and potentially harmful disillusionment must be laid to Watergate.

Of course it may not all be Watergate. Maybe it's partially Watergate and partially the fact that some of today's high school teachers were burning the college campuses as students in the late sixties.

Here's an illustration. Last spring students at Walt Whitman High School in Bethesda, Maryland, were supposed to study Chinese history for nine weeks. One teacher used the opportunity to experiment with a Marxist indoctrination of two dozen students. They began each class session performing calisthenics before a bigger than life poster of Lenin. The teacher, who led the exercises, admitted he had drifted to the left of American liberalism and planned to enroll in a Marxist study group. He taught Chinese history from a Maoist viewpoint, complete with the calisthenics, recitations from Chairman Mao, and the selection of an appropriate slogan for the day from Mao's little red book. Two-thirds of the final grade was based on self and group criticism and how well the student accepted it. The other third was a written examination testing the degree to which the students properly displayed the Maoist political view.

I wonder how many of the parents in that district bothered to vote in the last school board election?

Watergate might have a long range cathartic effect on politics in the United States by eliminating the moral double standard by which politics has traditionally been practiced. While I've never believed in a double standard in politics or anything else, we have to recognize it's there. Even people who are the soul of honor and honesty have come to expect politics and politicians to operate on a looser moral standard. It isn't that honest people have approved of political immorality; they've just accepted it as necessary. They sum it up in the old line: "That's politics."

The traditional immorality of politics is no defense of Watergate. The fact that worse things may have happened under other presidents can't be used as an excuse. It's obvious, though, that the press wouldn't have been as interested in Watergate if the Democrats had been the culprits, which in itself is an indictment against the morality even of those who ferreted out the Watergate immorality. They weren't objectively ferreting out immorality; they were trying to prove that the faction they disagreed with had played "dirty tricks" on the faction they supported.

The halls of government ought to be nearly as sacred to the people and their leaders as a church or cathedral or temple. And the press ought to ferret out political immorality with consistent vigor, no matter where the chips fall. Some people think that wouldn't leave many professional politicians. Maybe they're right, and maybe that wouldn't be such a bad result.

Traditionally the American political system has been a two-party system. Recently it has moved toward a no-party system, as the registration in both major parties declines and more and more people come to consider themselves "independents." Either the parties are growing out of touch with people, or the people misunderstand the parties.

We in the Republican Party have two problems. First, we haven't been able to shake the image the liberals created for us 40 years ago, the "fat-cat" image, with dollar signs on our vests. Second, some Republicans have looked at the success of the Democratic Party—presidents in 28 and congressional control in 41 of the past 43 years—and decided we should be more like them. As a result, many people refuse to associate or work with either party, since they can't see a difference.

It's silly as well as dishonest to imitate the Democrats. They've given away so much of the store that they haven't discovered the people don't like the goods anymore. A survey done by Georgetown University shows clearly the people's disaffection with the policies of the Democratic Party. Georgetown's Political Science Department polled the 1972 Democratic and Republican convention delegates on the major issues. Then they polled rank and file members of the Democratic Party. They found that rank and file Democrats were in almost perfect agreement with the positions of the Republican delegates and poles apart from the positions of their own delegates.

The object lesson for Republicans is to stop whimpering "me-too" after every statement by the Democrats, even to stop trying to sell Republicanism, and concentrate on stating their beliefs simply and clearly.

135

The position of women in American society has recently been revived as an important political issue. Although the elements of what has been called the "women's liberation movement" have been disparate in their views on many subjects, they have generally rallied to the support of the proposed Equal Rights Amendment (E.R.A.) to the Constitution, which states simply, "Equality of rights under the law shall not be denied or abridged by the United States or by any State on account of sex."

I'm for equal rights for women, but I'm not for the Equal Rights Amendment, a position my own daughter finds hard to believe. When I first read the E.R.A., I supported it. On first reading, it appeared to be a clear and simple statement of equal rights. But the results of the last couple of years of legal research have convinced me that the E.R.A. is not as simple as it appears.

I firmly believe that equal work demands equal pay, regardless of sex. I firmly believe that jobs should be awarded on the basis of merit and not sex. I am convinced that where brains and common sense are the criteria, women are as able as men.

But I still don't like the E.R.A.

I believe the E.R.A. would take away laws that were passed especially to make sure that women were not put upon by men. Divorce laws, for example, and child support laws. Laws protecting women from being forced to work long hours at hard physical labor. Rape laws.

I also believe the E.R.A. would force the United States in case of war not only to draft women but also to put them in combat, alongside men, where they would undergo the same physical hardships and brutal experiences. I don't want that for women.

And the E.R.A. could be interpreted by some judges in ways that would degrade and defeminize women by forcing them to mingle with men in close, intimate quarters. I don't want to see—and I don't believe most Americans want to see—rest-

rooms, barracks, and shower rooms integrated sexually.

Human beings are not animals, and I do not want to see sex and sexual differences treated as casually and amorally as dogs and other beasts treat them. I believe this could happen under E.R.A.

These are personal reasons. There are legal reasons, too, for my opposition. There's nothing in the present Constitution that says women are not equal to men. Congress and the states can, and do, legislate to correct inequities and, indeed, to ensure that women who choose to be housewives and full-time mothers are protected. But if we adopt the E.R.A., we will have given the legislative power completely to the federal government. State laws and the right of states to legislate in this area will be done away with.

Today, if you don't like the laws in your state you can move. When the federal government takes control, there is no place to move to.

Not long ago I was interviewed by a woman who asked if my wife Nancy is liberated. I told her I wasn't sure what she meant. "Well," she said, "is Nancy just your wife or does she have a life of her own?" I told her that we think of ourselves as a team. Nancy doesn't need liberating because she doesn't think of herself as being my chattel in any way. She made up her own mind that marriage was a career in itself, and she does darned well at it.

We should never forget that women are the civilizing influence of our society. If it weren't for the influence of women, men would still be carrying clubs. You can easily observe the coarseness that comes over a group of men removed, for any reason, from the feminine influence.

I think women should play a much larger role in government. I think they'd tend to be more realistic and candid, that they'd expect people to take care of themselves more. I think there would be fewer elaborate systems for government interference. Maybe the trouble with those professional "women's libbers" I mentioned earlier is related to something Will Rogers once said, "If women go on trying to be more and more equal to men, someday they won't know any more than men do."

Although today's dissatisfaction with government is not new, it is perhaps more widespread and intense than at any time in the past 100 years. Yet never before has any government made such expensive and grandoise attempts to meet its people's needs. The lesson is clear: a paternalistic government—no matter how benevolent—and individual liberty, the heart of American democracy, are incompatible.

The people's instincts are still right. You see them come to the rescue of someone—a child who falls down a well—hundreds of people rush to help, and labor and equipment are volunteered without any thought of who's going to pay for it. This is a basic feeling in Americans. They don't stand back in such a circumstance and ask what government's going to do about it.

The parable of the good Samaritan sums it up. The story isn't about how unfortunate the pilgrim is who's been beaten and robbed and left to die by the side of the road. The story is about the virtue of the Samaritan who didn't pass the pilgrim by, who stopped, bound up his wounds, carried him to an inn, saw to it that he was cared for, and paid for that care.

I think the travelers who ignored the pilgrim are the people who today take the attitude of "Let the government do it." The Samaritan recognized that the pilgrim's problem was a human problem, not a government problem.

Democracy without Bureaucracy?

Ronald Reagan's idea of a workable democracy is one in which bureaucracy does not come between the people and their leaders. Realistically, democracy in America hinges upon the reduction and decentralization of government, leading to a more direct and candid relationship, at all levels of government, between elected officials and the people who elected them. **"Let the people understand. Because the people's instincts are still right."**

Being a government planner in a free society should be almost as unrewarding as being a free-thinker in a fascist state. The major difference, as any bureaucrat can tell you, is that while a free society may thwart your plans, it allows you to keep your job and your life. The resulting combination of frustration and security gives government planners an attitude of desperate benevolence toward the people they serve. They want to tell us how to live and, by heaven, we'd better listen if we know what's good for us.

Unfortunately, their compulsion to make us listen often turns planners into schemers, looking for ways to make us live as they think we should, whether we like it or not. Their latest scheme, shaped and polished over the past 15 years, is a new layer of government, called "regional government."

The idea of regional government really stems

from the bureaucrats' distrust of elected officials and the people who elected them. Elected officials sometimes listen to the people, much to the distress of the planners. The answer: reduce the power of elected officials, and thus of the people, by installing regional governments of appointed bureaucrats to make all of the important decisions. The design: put regional governments between local and state governments to usurp local control, and put other regional governments between the states and the federal government to usurp states' rights.

Regionalists have tried to disguise the movement toward regionalism as a public good in two ways, both spurious.

The first is the argument that state and local governments, and especially our larger cities, have failed to meet the public needs of their citizens. The argument is persuasive until one looks at the incredible burden that Washington has placed on state and local governments. With its ability to deficit spend, the federal government has forced lower levels of government into so-called sharing programs that have broken the backs of local taxpayers and placed impossible restrictions on the flexibility of local governments.

The second approach has been for regionalists to join with environmentalists in promoting a myth that only regional governments can solve regional problems, such as pollution, congestion, and transportation. This contention presupposes that there are natural geopolitical "regions" in which all of these problems are completely contained. The truth is that each problem affects a unique area and population, making boundaries for general purpose regional governments as artificial as state and county boundaries. These problems are best solved by cooperation of local governments—cooperation forced by the state, if necessary.

One of the calling cards of the regionalists across the country is a lapel button labeled *"Be regionable."* You'll see it at meetings of regional government advocates. What does it mean? It means, "We're big government and we know what's best for you. To get it, all you have to do is give up some of your liberty. Now, 'be regionable'—and give it to us."

Just as it would be folly to put bureaucrats into decision-making positions in regional governments, so it would be equally foolish to leave federal bureaucrats in positions where they are called upon to make judgments beyond their knowledge and competence. Regulations from Washington, D.C., are often inappropriate, sometimes ludicrous.

Here's an example of what happens when government becomes a monopoly and the bureaucrats are free to inflict their wills on the rest of us. HEW decided last year that it should check into the facilities and operations of hospitals getting federal money. In checking, the inspectors found that many hospitals are using plastic liners in the wastebaskets, and HEW insisted they be removed, because if they caught fire they would produce toxic fumes. But the federal Occupational Safety and Health Administration (OSHA) has demanded that the bags be there to protect employees from contamination when the wastebaskets are emptied. What are the hospitals supposed to do: put the bags in for OSHA and take them out when HEW comes around?

For 40 years the government has created programs that are supposed to help people. The average American is generous, and his natural initial response to these programs has been "Sure, I'm for that, if it's going to help someone who needs it." But the government then creates a bureaucracy to run the program and the bureaucracy completely eliminates the personal involvement of the people.

The poor beleaguered citizen watches his taxes

go up and wonders why all those people who were supposed to be helped are complaining. He's been shut out from helping them, but he's sure he could do a better job of it than the government, for far less money. The government has only taken his money to pay people to be poor. As Milton Friedman has said, "If you pay people to be poor, there are going to be a lot of poor people." Charity has been made both impersonal and ineffective by assigning it to government bureaucracy.

Plumas County, a small rural county in northern California, decided last year that it had had enough of bureaucracy. In an unprecedented move, it announced that it was not going to participate any longer in the federal and state welfare programs. One of its reasons was that the administrative overhead, dictated by federal and state regulations, was taking a third of every welfare dollar.

Innovation is almost unknown in a bureaucracy. In older bureaucracies, such as those that have existed in European nations for scores and sometimes hundreds of years, innovation is considered heretical deviation. Reagan explains the dangers of military bureaucracies.

We've been very successful in fighting wars, when we had to, with civilian control and with citizen soldiers serving only temporarily in the military. We've never built up a great European-style military bureaucracy.

And our system has proved to be the best. The traditional military bureaucracies have always been most interested in using their tools and their strategies. The attitude of the American army has always been: "Let's get this thing over with so we can go home and do what we want to." We haven't been militarily bookbound. In World War I the European generals knew what their opponents would do because they all had read the same books. They weren't prepared for a bunch of Americans whose logic was simply, "Where are they and how do we get at them?"

Whatever the rationalizations for creating and perpetuating bureaucracies, in the final analysis all of them founder on thrift. Limited funds result in limited bureaucracies. Tightening the government's fiscal belt is a sure way to produce a bureaucratic weight loss.

The most effective thing that can be done to improve government is to limit permanently the amount of money it gets, a limit determined as a percentage of what all the people together earn, a limit determined on the basis that no more than that amount should be available to our public servants to perform public functions. In a society as complex as ours, in a world as prone to totalitarianism as ours has proved to be, limited government is our best guarantee of continued freedom.

We simply have to cut government off at the pockets.

Part II

The Record

How Ronald Reagan
Governed California*

The previous chapters have presented the philosophy of
Ronald Reagan—his concept of a realistic democracy—in
his own words. But given the structure of American
government today, how well can Reagan or any executive
implement such beliefs? As it happens, we have a demon-
stration of Reagan's political abilities in his governorship
of California. The following chapter is an assessment of
that governorship.

An appraisal of Ronald Reagan as governor of California should start with the 1971 welfare reform negotiations between his administration and the liberal
Democrats who controlled the California Legislature. The
objective of the negotiations was to construct a welfare
reform act, the legislative component of Reagan's
celebrated welfare reform program. The Reagan team had
just detected some legal "quicksand" in the language
drafted by the legislature's staff. If left in the bill, the
language would undo a major element of the reform that
Reagan had proposed and Assembly Speaker Bob Moretti,
under tremendous public pressure, had reluctantly agreed
to. The legislators and their staff members, opposed to
any welfare reform at all and trying hard to soften its
impact, argued that the language was inconseqeuntial;
the Reagan team insisted that the wording be changed to

*This article by Charles Hobbs originally appeared in the *National
Review* January 17, 1975, pages 28-42. Reprinted by permission.

reflect the Reagan-Moretti agreement. An impasse was reached and one of the legislators, whose self-appointed role was to maintain an atmosphere that would encourage compromise, called for a recess and sent for food and drink. Warmed by his own hospitality and trying to put the situation in perspective, he commented: "It's too bad the people elect an ideologue like Reagan. They should stick with political whores, like me." His candor broke the ice and negotiations were resumed; the questionable language was redrafted to satisfy the "ideologue."

For anyone who takes seriously Ronald Reagan's 1965 statement that "nothing is more opposed to creativeness than bureaucracy," the chronicling of his governorship of California might be expected to recall the Battle of Gettysburg. That it doesn't is a credit to Reagan as a man. He had the best opportunity in our time to test the practical value of the conservative principles underlying the belief that uncontrolled growth and power of government are the greatest threat to our freedom and, therefore, to our nation and lives. He consciously strove to take advantage of that opportunity, and the future usefulness of these principles depends upon our willingness to examine honestly and critically the outcome of Reagan's eight years as leader of the largest and most typical of the United States. I hope that this article will serve as the beginning of that examination.

There are three impediments to such an examination. The first is the uncertainty produced, or at least reinforced, by the national events of the last six months—Nixon's resignation, his pardon by Ford, Rockefeller's ordeal as he sought the Vice Presidency, and the prospect of a full scale repression. It is an awkward time to analyze a current political career.

The second impediment is the budding crop of superficial appraisals celebrating the retirement of California's "citizen-politician." Clearly California and Reagan are parting friends, and the consensus, except at the raveled fringes of the political fabric, is that both have profited, but the state more so, from their eight-year association. California enters 1975 with a constantly decreasing welfare population receiving constantly increasing benefits;

with financially and technically sound energy and water supply systems; with enforced environmental standards that are both lowering air and water pollution and preserving an extraordinary range of recreational opportunities; with a superb highway system that has become an orderly segment of an integrated transportation system responsive to both state and local needs; with $1 billion in property tax relief funds disbursed each year to local governments; with no more state employees than eight years ago, even though in that time state spending has doubled and state services have multiplied; with a public university system in which teaching, learning, and research have replaced violent confrontation and preparation for armed revolution; and with a $500-million budget surplus to buffer California against the coming hard times.

Even Reagan's enemies will agree, publicly if they can afford to and privately if they can't, that these assets are mainly the products of the personal and political strength, vision, and persistence of Ronald Reagan. That is why, as this article is being written, journalists like Lou Cannon of the *Washington Post* and Tom Goff of the *Los Angeles Times* have already published positive assessments of Reagan's performance as governor. Their theme seems to be that "he did a lot better than most of us thought he would." Heady praise from a generally liberal working press—unless one realizes that even the most liberal of the Sacramento press corps has succumbed to Reagan's unique combination of charm, intelligence, and integrity, and until one remembers that most of the people who try to mold others' opinions considered him, in 1966, a woefully inexperienced and unintelligent reactionary, preprogrammed and made up to look like a gubernatorial candidate by Hollywood, Madison Avenue, and the money men of Southern California. Pat Brown, the incumbent governor, underestimated both the voters and Reagan and lost to him by almost a million votes. Only the people saw and understood in 1966 that Reagan wrote his own speeches and meant what he said. The opinion leaders are just now catching up with the people.

The third and most difficult impediment in appraising

Ronald Reagan's performance is the conservative's desire to find his administration faultless or, avoiding that gross pitfall, to see what flaws there are through conservatively tinted glasses. Watching the rising tide of bureaucracy, we are tempted to succumb to the vision of the man on the white horse. Mythology is full of such would-be national saviors, like the mad Irish hero Cuchulain who tried to beat back the sea with his sword. Reagan is Irish as well as conservative. Only four months ago he said, "I have also learned that politics, which is often called the second oldest profession, has a great similiarity to the first."

We must ask the hard questions, not only about Reagan the man, but about Reagan the governor. How well did he put into practice the principles he enunciated so well just before the 1964 election in his famous "speech"? Did his accomplishments match his plans, or was he forced to bend principles to meet the political realities of a state that transacts more business than all but six or seven nations? Was he able to attract people to develop programs consistent with his principles? How often was he blocked from even greater accomplishments by people who, although personally loyal, either did not understand how or did not share the desire to reduce to practice his principles? How effective was he in the give and take of political warfare, where compromise is supposedly the only way to succeed? How well did he manage a large bureaucracy while admittedly holding views strongly antithetical to bureaucratic purposes and practices? Finally, is there any meaning in his experience for the future of conservation and, if so, what is it?

Three facets of Reagan's personality have colored and often controlled his decisions and impact as governor. First there is his charm: very few people, alone or in a group, can meet or listen to Reagan without liking him. He is at once interesting and interested—as good a listener as he is a talker—and the effect of his personal magnetism cannot be disregarded.

The second important facet of his personality is his integrity in adhering to his principles, no matter what the circumstances. The Davis University students who applauded him at a recent rally were also applauding Reagan's ability, courage, and readiness to express his principles, politely but firmly, to an audience he knew had been conditioned to disagree with him. In my research and experience there is no instance in which he had compromised his principles for personal or political gain. He came intellectually prepared to Sacramento, to the amazement of his critics and even some of his supporters, with a well thought out political philosophy and a matching set of principles from which he has never deviated.

Unfortunately, the third and least publicly understood facet of his personality has often undone the effects of the first two. For better or worse, Ronald Reagan is the most compassionate person I have ever met. Nor am I alone in this assessment: his closest advisers are both awed and dismayed by Reagan's inability to inflict injury on, or tolerate injury to, other people, except people who have harmed or injured a third party. Not only can't he hurt another person; he has great difficulty in withdrawing even a part of the complete trust he invariably places in those who work for him, even when their actions publicly embarrass him.

As a society we have come to expect our political leaders to be, to a certain degree, Janus-faced. Thinking it through, most of us would probably wonder how else a politician could both get votes and manage a government agency. Ronald Reagan doesn't change personalities when he turns from the TV cameras and enters his private office. Peel off the layers of formality that he adds for his public appearances and you find only an increasingly informal version of the same person. In fact, the more informal the setting, the more his natural compassion and consideration for others surface. That is why people who expect to hate Reagan find, on meeting him, that they like him. "He attracts all kinds of people," Jim Jenkins, one of Reagan's closest policy advisers, told me, and added that screening Reagan's visitors was important only because "we were always afraid the next one would come out wearing the Governor's shirt."

Reagan's undeviating loyalty to his subordinates, even to those who could not or would not put his principles into practice, has produced failures and missed opportunities that, in fairness, must be chalked up against him. On the other hand, when his subordinates have shared his principles and had the courage and ability to design and carry out programs based on those principles, Reagan has proved not only that conservatism in government can work, but that in practice it represents the will of the vast majority of Americans of all backgrounds.

In 1967 Reagan inherited an incredible fiscal mess: the product of clumsy attempts by Pat Brown's outgoing administration to prevent either a major tax increase or severe program cutbacks in an election year. Brown's director of finance, Hale Champion, informed Reagan's incoming staff that the 1966 to 1967 budget was running a deficit of $1 million a day, wished them good luck, and walked out. The entire Medi-Cal (California's greatly expanded version of Medicaid) budget for the year had been spent in the six months before Reagan became governor. The statewide water system was severely underfunded because the value of the bonds to finance the project had been set at what Brown thought could win voter approval, a value far short of the actual construction costs of the system. In short, Reagan entered Sacramento, scalpel in hand, prepared to trim away the excess fat of government spending, only to find that he already had a $200-million budget deficit, a commitment for a water system that was underfunded by another several hundred millions of dollars, and a $4-billion potentially unfunded liability, in the State Teacher's Retirement System that, if not quickly corrected, would balloon local property tax rates.

In his first year as governor he was forced to raise state taxes by $900 million. But before he left office eight years later he had returned more than $1 billion of state taxes directly to the citizens of California and was providing another $1 billion per year in local property tax relief in the form of subventions to local governments to be spent for local programs. A miracle? Definitely not. A significant accomplishment? The answer can only be a qualified yes, considering that during the same period of time the state budget doubled and state spending grew at one and a half times the rate of state personal income. State taxes actually grew faster under Reagan than under Brown, but that was mainly the result of Brown's sleight of hand shift in the state accounting system from cash to accrual and toleration of a growing budget deficit during his last year in office.

Ronald Reagan wanted, much more than his predecessor, to control overall spending but, like his predecessor, was unable to do so. For at least the past 20 years the governor and the legislature have maintained only a semblance of control over the budget and expenditures of the State of California. Control has actually been balanced between two bureaucratic agencies, neither of which has been held directly accountable to the people. These agencies are the state Department of Finance, ostensibly reporting to the governor and charged with preparing the annual governor's budget for submission to the legislature, and the Office of the Legislative Analyst, ostensibly reporting to the legislature for the primary purpose of analyzing the adequacy and quality of the governor's budget. By playing off executive departments against each other, by helping to ensure that elected critics get enough funds, or economies, or programs to keep them happy, by maintaining staffs with superior knowledge of the budget process, these two agencies have acted as an informal coalition in controlling the lion's share of California's budget, and with it California's expenditures and taxes. The symbolic relationship of the two agencies has made the Department of Finance bureaucracy so strong that, as Ned Hutchinson, Reagan's highly respected appointments secretary for six years, said, "Unfortunately, we never laid a glove on them." They gave the conservative governor what he wanted: tax refunds to the people and property tax relief for local government. They gave the liberal legislature what it wanted: more money for more state programs. But they kept effective control of the budget—their primary goal; and the secondary goal thus defined itself: increases in taxes and government spending that would allow them to satisfy their "customers"—the governor and the legislature.

Ned Hutchinson was drafted into the Reagan administration, as were many of those who became administration stalwarts, through the Businessmen's Task Force, Reagan's first major attempt at reform of the bureaucracy. Borrowing the idea from Governor James Rhodes of Ohio, Reagan recruited some 250 businessmen from the major industries of the state. Speaking to small groups of business leaders about the reforms he had promised in his campaign, he would wait until his audience began, one by one, to pull out their checkbooks. Then he would say: "I don't need your money, I need your talent. There's a sign-up sheet by the door. If you can spare a day, a week, a month, or more, please sign up as you leave." The response was overwhelming, and for ten months, from February to December 1967, the state's most successful businessmen looked critically over the shoulders of its civil servants.

It turned out to be as much an audit as a reform (although most of the task force's 1,500 recommendations were eventually implemented, and many resulted in substantial cost savings), but a greater benefit was the business community's better understanding of the problems and challenges of managing the nation's largest state. Many successful businessmen, like Hutchinson, stayed to be a part of Reagan's management team. In fact, Hutchinson first coordinated the implementation of the recommendations, and graduated from that laborious task to the even more difficult one of picking candidates for the 300-odd political appointments Reagan controlled. "There were always plenty of qualified and experienced people available," says Hutchinson, "but not enough of them also shared the Governor's conservative principles and zeal to implement those principles."

From the start Reagan operated through an executive assistant, who functioned more or less as assistant governor. The first of these, Philip Battaglia, a dynamic Los Angeles attorney, left less than a year after Reagan took office. The second was William Clark, also an attorney, now a justice on the California Supreme Court. Reagan and Clark began, in late 1967 and early 1968, to apply the business management techniques that Reagan had promised to bring to state government, and that the

Businessmen's Task Force had given shape. Reagan and Clark set up a cabinet that would be a forum for threshing out policy positions on the multitude of expensive, complex, overlapping, and sometimes almost invisible state programs. Each cabinet member, except the executive secretary, was also secretary of an agency comprising several functional departments. There were four such agencies: Human Relations (later Health and Welfare), Business and Transportation, Agriculture and Services, and Resources. The agency secretaries usually exercised no direct-line management responsibility except when their programs were in experimental or developmental stages, when they would be most susceptible to technical and political criticism. Under the cabinet system the line departments would make their budget requests to the agency secretaries, who would then meet with the governor and argue the case for the fiscal needs of their agencies. Then the cabinet, headed by the governor, would set spending priorities and limits and instruct the Department of Finance as to what should constitute the governor's budget.

In retrospect, it appears that Reagan, Clark, and the other cabinet members did not know how strong a grip the old-line bureaucrats of the Department of Finance had on the preparation and enactment of the budget, or how close they came to breaking that grip with the establishment of the governor's cabinet. What saved the bureaucracy was its technical expertise. The new cabinet secretaries could not fathom the governor's budget, a document so esoteric that nowhere in it can be found the first requirement of any budget: single numbers representing the total projected expenditures of the state treasury for the current year and for the projected year. Technical help obviously was needed: the director of finance was added to the cabinet as a full-fledged member and, properly briefed by his indulgent civil service staff, continued to call the shots. For the past five and a half years the director of finance has been Verne Orr, a man who is universally liked and respected by the state legislators and in whom Reagan has always placed great trust. Orr has been totally loyal to Reagan but, like other directors of finance before him, has depended completely for technical support on the civil servants who have managed the budget for over twenty years.

The cabinet worked well in other ways, however. A cabinet secretary would act as a sergeant at arms and parliamentarian, keeping the discussion as close to the agenda topic as possible. The structured discussion of cabinet issues, summarized before the meetings in "Cabinet Issue Memos," and the open exchange of views among all of Reagan's top advisers, with his active participation, were a vast improvement on the practices of his predecessors, who had usually decided issues on the advice of whoever was present at the time—cabinet member, legislator, lobbyist, or old fraternity brother. The cabinet made a workable routine for the day-to-day policy management of the executive branch. Had Pat Brown had such a forum, some of the disasters that struck his administration might have been averted, or at least reduced in effect. One such disaster was the decline and fall of the University of California in 1964.

A question that conservatives should ask about Ronald Reagan is why the vast majority of college and university students in California think he belongs in one of the lower levels of the Inferno. Part of the answer may be that most college students don't want to like or believe any public figure, on the assumption that to be a public figure is probably to be a hypocrite. But then most people, including most college students, are hypocrites, and Ronald Reagan, despite the political cartoonists, is not.

In addition Reagan has made no effort to communicate directly with large groups of college students, mainly because some of the staff members who scheduled his speaking engagements felt that student audiences would invariably contain provocateurs, and most students wouldn't vote anyway.

But for one who knows what Ronald Reagan believes in and how close, notwithstanding the generation gap, his beliefs are to what most students say they want to believe in, neither answer is satisfactory. I think the larger part of the answer lies in the insecurity and paranoia of the University of California's administration and faculty, stemming from its public attempt at self-destruction as an institution of higher learning in 1964. The spectacle of the president of one of the most respected institutions of higher learning in the world bargaining away, in exchange for a campus police car, administrative control of the university to a few hundred radical faculty and student punks, destroyed almost instantaneously California's respect for its university. When, two years later, Ronald Reagan became the spokesman for a free society faced by a revolution fomented on the campuses, his targets, whether he willed it or not, were students. He realizes, and has said so over and over again, that the real culprits in campus unrest are a few students swayed by a radical minority of the faculty. But the wall between Reagan and students is there, and it is only recently that Reagan himself has shown the inclination to climb over or walk around that wall. The students, having more pride than experience, will stay on their side until he comes over to be tested.

Another wall is the wall between him and some members of the California Supreme Court, particularly the Chief Justice he appointed in 1970, Donald Wright. Soon after he took office, Reagan initiated a system by which candidates for judgeships would be prescreened and evaluated by committees composed of members of the bar, judges, and laymen before he personally selected from among the candidates. He also applied a rule of thumb to his selection of judicial candidates: whenever possible, he would try to appoint judges who were younger than 55, so that the state legal system could benefit from the store of experience they would gather.

Reagan's system for appointing judges and his judicial appointments have been hailed as exceptionally good by conservatives, and even liberals admit that the quality of judicial appointments has improved under Reagan. For Reagan and other conservatives, however, Donald Wright has been a tragic disappointment as Chief Justice of the State Supreme Court, which had for years been somewhat to the left of even the Warren Court. Wright was expected to help remedy that tilt, and his conversations with Reagan prior to his appointment reinforced that expectation. Reagan fudged a bit on his rule of thumb: Wright was 63, but he had mentioned, in several conversations with Reagan's advisers, that he intended to retire on his twentieth anniversary as a judge, which would occur before the end of Reagan's second term and allow Reagan then to appoint a younger man. Reagan also thought that Wright supported the death penalty.

Reagan made Wright Chief Justice, and Wright changed colors overnight. He wrote the decision abolishing the death penalty in California, voted with the Brown-appointed liberals on most issues, and, instead of retiring, he sought and gained reconfirmation in the last general election. The wall between Reagan and Wright is probably a permanent one.

The cabinet, however valuable as a management forum and a stimulant to intelligent decision making, was still basically a reactive, not an innovative mechanism, and Reagan was more interested in changing government than in just managing it. He firmly believes that government should be out of most of the businesses it has gotten into since 1930, and that the private sector should be increasing, not decreasing, its role in solving society's problems. Before William Clark left to become a judge in early 1969, he fathered a Program Development Office within the governor's office for the specific purpose of developing innovative programs that would lessen the intervention of the state government in people's lives and pocketbooks. The office generated many ideas and went a long way toward explaining, in terms of specific program, what the "Creative Society" government could accomplish. The office's proposals, however, were never equipped with implementing mechanisms.

In a more specific attempt at reducing government expansion, Reagan's staff took aim, early in 1970, at the California Rural Legal Assistance agency, a group of attorneys, set up by the federal Office of Economic Opportunity (OEO) to give legal assistance to the poor, but under the administrative control of the state OEO, which was headed by Lew Uhler, a Reagan appointee. Uhler's aides began to build a file showing that CRLA attorneys were organizing protests against the government that was paying them, in violation of the regulations covering their scope of work. Reagan, relying on what seemed to be massive and well documented evidence presented by Uhler, vetoed CRLA funds for the coming year. In Washington, Frank Carlucci, then OEO director, holding that the Reagan charges could not be substantiated, indicated he would override the veto. Reagan sought the backing of President Nixon, and a thorough investigation of the charges ensued. As it turned out, the staff work done for Reagan was inadequate. A few of the charges held up, but most, although probably true, could not be substantiated by hard evidence, and Reagan was forced to back off. In a no-win, no-lose compromise, CRLA got half the money it had expected, and the other half went to the state to create a new legal aid program for the poor, which, however, never got off the ground.

Reagan was learning from these mistakes. He finally developed the mechanism that was to turn the thrust of his administration from simply improving government management to improving government itself when, in mid-1970, he found that uncontrolled growth of the welfare system threatened to bankrupt the state.

In the spring of 1971 Ronald Reagan singlehandedly cleaned up the federally created "welfare mess" in his state by (1) restricting welfare to those who really needed it, (2) increasing the benefits to those truly in need, and (3) requiring able-bodied welfare recipients either to take a job for pay or perform public services for their welfare grants. These simple steps, implemented through an elaborate, carefully timed series of administrative directors from his Director of Social Welfare, Robert Carleson, to California's 58 County Welfare Departments, produced immediate and to the rest of the nation, incredible results: within 30 days the welfare case load, which had been growing at a rate of 25,000 to 40,000 persons per month, leveled off and began to drop. It has dropped ever since, and there are now 400,000 fewer people on welfare in California than there were in February, 1971.

Savings in state and local taxes, by the most conservative estimates, are more than $2 billion, with another

$2-billion saving in federal taxes. And, most galling to liberals who said it couldn't be done, welfare grants, after an initial 30% increase as part of the reform, have continued to rise with the cost of living, so that no Californian on welfare will be penalized by inflation. Nor was this welfare reform fortuitous: every other large state's welfare case load continued to grow while California's fell until one by one the other states, led by New York, with Governor Nelson Rockefeller publicly toasting Reagan on his success, came to California to learn the formula for welfare reform. Reagan's welfare reform director, Robert Carleson, has since become federal Commissioner of Welfare, and serves as HEW'S representative to states with runaway welfare problems.

Many conservatives know about these simple and impressive results, but few know how the combination of knowledge, creativity, courage, and perseverance that produced those results was brought about. Even fewer realize that those results were achieved despite the active and concentrated opposition of the Nixon Administration, of HEW, of the organized federal, state and local welfare bureaucracies, of the California Legislature, of every special interest group involved, and even of the bureaucratically controlled portion of Reagan's own administration.

The story really started in the early autumn of 1969, when President Nixon and his staff humanitarian, Pat Moynihan, were trying to sell the Congress and the governors on the Family Assistance Program (FAP better expresses the qualities of its subject than any other acronym in my experience). By then Ed Meese, an ex-deputy district attorney of Alameda County, and a man who, as legal affairs secretary, had already shown himself to be not only absolutely loyal to Reagan but a master at gaining consensus within the cabinet, had replaced William Clark as Reagan's executive secretary. At the Western White House in San Clemente, Reagan and Meese listened to FAP described in Moynihan's honeyed brogue. Welfare recipients would benefit; states would benefit; the "welfare mess" would be cleaned up once and for all, and by a national Republican Administration. Reagan and Meese were almost convinced.

In Washington, however, Jim Jenkins, then Reagan's "ambassador" to the Federal Government, was seeing a slightly different picture. Jenkins passed his information along to Reagan. Reading the reports himself and knowing the liberal crew that was writing the bill, Jenkins came to the conclusion that FAP would probably turn out to be another giant step toward state socialism in the form of a guaranteed federal dole to workers and non-workers alike, sugarcoated with savings for states but hiding an enormous price tag that would force a federal income tax increase or an expansion of the national debt. Jenkins flew to Sacramento, and briefed Reagan and the cabinet on what FAP would really be with Moynihan's rhetoric peeled away. Between Jenkins' briefing and the intensive discussion that followed, Reagan probably received more information about the potential effects of FAP than Nixon ever did. On the evidence, this time meticulously researched, Reagan concluded that California could not support the President and that FAP would, if implemented, be a burden the nation could not bear. A few months later, in the summer of 1970, Reagan made his first and only appearance before Congress as governor of California when he testified at length to Senator Russell Long's Finance Committee as to how and why, in his opinion, FAP would be a disaster for his state and for the nation. Even as he spoke, he realized that, as governor of the largest state, his best hope of stopping FAP would be to design a workable alternative. From this realization California's Welfare Reform Program was born.

Returning to Sacramento, Reagan formed a task force of experts in law, public administration, and business management, expressly picking people who had had no previous experience of, and therefore had no stake in, the current welfare system. Under the leadership of Ned Hutchinson, this team spent five months examining the welfare system to see if it could be changed to make people less, rather than more, dependent on government handouts. The Welfare Reform Task Force concluded not only that such changes could be made, but that simultaneously aid to the needy could be increased and the cost of the system reduced.

The welfare crisis had not only elicited a workable reform program but discovered a mechanism—the independent task force of experts relieved from day to day management responsibilities—for determining how to make those permanent changes in government for which Reagan had campaigned and been elected.

In laying out for Reagan their detailed plans for welfare reform, the task force members, to a man, expressed their doubts that the legislature would enact the parts of the plan that could not be carried out by executive fiat. Reagan disagreed, knowing that in this matter he held a trump card—the support of the people. Gambling that the initial administrative reforms, which he could order on his own authority through Carleson as state director of social welfare, would cause a sharp and immediate drop in case load growth, he felt the people would then agitate to force the legislature to complete the program.

Reagan won this one, but it was close. The attack began as soon as the legislature got Reagan's proposed 1971 to 1972 budget, with a marked decrease in funds for welfare. A. Alan Post, the Legislative Analyst, immediately dubbed the proposed budget "the Property Tax Increase Act of 1971." He was wrong. Welfare reform worked: Forty-two of California's 58 counties lowered their property taxes that year, and Post's reputation for objectivity and accuracy suffered a severe setback.

But the legislature had other weapons. The annual legislative ritual of publicly massaging the governor's proposed budget for months and then appointing a six-man conference committee to formulate the legislature's counter-proposals offered an excellent opportunity to sabotage welfare reform. An integral, in fact critical, element in the welfare reform program was the administrative reorganization of the bureaucracy. That reorganization depended upon Carleson's having discretionary power through the budget to separate certain people from their old functions. The night before the completed budget was to be presented to and quickly passed by both houses of the legislature, so that it could be signed before the old year ended, members of the legislative staff changed enough of the budget control language to kill the reorganization. The new language was of a masterly obscurity, and its intent certainly would not normally have been noticed by members of the legislature.

Fortunately for Reagan, however, two members of his welfare reform team were also working late that night and decided to drop into the Capitol office where the budget document had just been "put to bed." An ebullient legislature aide, proud of the sabotage he and his companions had done to Reagan's plans, and thinking it too late for anyone to repair the damage, gleefully spilled the beans.

Early the next morning each member of Reagan's welfare reform team approached key legislators, one by one, as they entered the budget session, pointing out the change in wording and the effect it would have, not only on welfare reform, but on future governors' abilities to organize the executive branch. Before the budget was passed, both houses had passed resolutions upholding Carleson's right to reorganize his department. One of the most liberal and influential of the Democratic senators took it upon himself to sponsor and personally ensure passage of a budget revision bill, undoing the sabotage and permitting the reorganization to be accomplished.

Finally, the efforts of the welfare reform team, combined with the overwhelming reactions of the public, brought Assembly Speaker Bob Moretti to the point of surrender. Appearing at Reagan's office door he held up his hands and said: "Stop the cards and letters. I'm ready to negotiate a welfare reform act." So, in August 1971, after Reagan had been in office four and a half years, the legislature realized that Reagan was a governor as well as an ideologue.

Reagan had been reelected in 1970, beating Jesse Unruh by half a million votes. The margin would probably have been much greater had not Reagan, again showing the compassion that is, for him, a principle in itself, spent the last weeks of the campaign stumping for his old and ill friend George Murphy who, even so, lost his Senate seat to John Tunney. Reagan, who had always said that eight years was long enough for anybody to be governor, announced immediately after his reelection that he would not run for a third term. By then even legislators were beginning to understand that Reagan always kept his word, so throughout the crucial days of welfare reform Reagan was acting from a lame-duck position.

Negotiations for the waivers of the Social Security Act that would give federal blessing to welfare reform were conducted principally with John Venerman, assistant secretary of HEW, a former California Republican assemblyman and close friend of Robert Finch, Reagan's first lieutenant governor. Despite this, Reagan's welfare reform team got a cool reception from Venerman and other HEW officials, many of whom felt that performing a public service for one's welfare grant was "slave labor." The negotiations dragged out for seven months, until the obvious success of the California program and the public enthusiasm it generated convinced HEW it could no longer stand in the way. HEW Secretary Elliot Richardson finally granted the Social Security Act waivers on August 3, 1972.

But the most unexpected opposition to welfare reform came from within the Reagan administration itself. Nearly a year after legislative approval of the Welfare Department reorganization, the state auditor general and the legislative counsel, both employees of the legislature, decided to investigate Welfare Department hiring practices. Charges of illegality against the Welfare Department during the reform battle were not unusual—Reagan, Carleson, and other officials had been defendants in some 140 suits filed mainly by CRLA attorneys—but in this case a new accuser was added. At a hearing called by the Assembly, the welfare reform team found itself accused of illegal and improper hiring practices, not only by the auditor general and legislative counsel, but also by representatives of Reagan's own Department of Finance, with the apparent knowledge and concurrence of Verne Orr, Reagan's appointed finance director. One of the members of the welfare reform team, remembering an old Pogo cartoon, muttered: "We have met the enemy, and they are us." The matter was resolved when State Attorney General Evelle Younger, independently elected and politically unaffected by welfare reform, ruled in favor of the Welfare Department. The last and cruelest attack on Reagan's welfare reform had been overcome. Looking back, the entire set of reforms had been designed and implemented, against overwhelming odds, by fewer than ten people, including the governor.

The welfare reform successes, precarious as they sometimes seemed to the small band of reformers, convinced Reagan that carefully constructed task forces, given the freedom and the authority to examine, could find conservative solutions to the problems of a large state government. In the spring of 1972 Reagan asked his cabinet to define the problems he should attempt to solve in his remaining three years in office. The cabinet decided upon three: crime in the streets, taxes, and the restructuring of local government. The Governor established two task forces immediately to address the problems of crime and taxes, and a year later created a final task force on local government.

The difference between the Task Force on Criminal Justice and the Task Force on Tax Reduction proved the diversity of the task force approach to government change. Reagan's executive secretary, Ed Meese, and his Criminal Justice Task Force produced a large number of relatively detailed and specific solutions that could be implemented, one by one, through legislation or administrative action by the state, or through individual actions by local governments. The recommendations ran the gamut from stiffer penalties for crimes of violence to methods of streamlining court procedures in order to reduce mounting case backlogs. This task force emulated the Welfare Reform Task Force in bringing together people from both inside and outside the administration, but differed slightly in its approach by recruiting individuals with extensive experience in law enforcement and court procedures. The positive impact of its recommendations, while not generating the publicity of welfare reform, will be felt for many years, at least in part

165

because its goal—the reduction of crime and restoration of safety for all Californians—is universally accepted.

On the other hand the Tax Reduction Task Force, headed by Lew Uhler, was charged to meet a goal with which many people, among them the majority of the legislature, did not agree: namely, to find a method for permanently reducing taxes and, coincidentally, the size and authority of government. One member of the task force, who had also been a principal designer of the welfare reform program, supplied the answer: a constitutional limitation on the portion of the total state personal income that the state government could take as revenue in any year and, since the task force thought that the current percentage was already too high, a provision for a slow rollback of the percentage until it reached the level it had been when Reagan became governor.

The concept was simple, much simpler than welfare reform; but because it dealt with the very heart of governmental power—the ability to tax—the task force knew from the start that such a program would be even harder to implement than welfare reform. First, the change would have to be constitutional, requiring a vote of the people. Second, the simplicity of the concept itself exposed the complexity of the state budget and expenditure process. Some state revenues went to a general fund, some to special funds for specific purposes, and some to funds over which the Federal Government exercised control. In addition, the state AAA bond rating and various government-subsidized pension programs would have to be protected. Most importantly, local governments would have to be insured against the state legislature's circumventing the revenue limit by transferring costs to local taxpayers. The problems associated with these complexities of the existing government structure would have to be resolved in the language of the proposed constitutional amendment, making it even harder for the voters to understand what they were voting for or against, especially in the face of campaign rhetoric.

Knowing these pitfalls, the task force sought the advice of more than two hundred economists, attorneys, political scientists, and other experts in national and state government finance to reduce the idea to its simplest workable form. Armed with the enthusiastic support of such eminent "government weight watchers" as Milton Friedman, Peter Drucker, C. Lowell Harriss, and James Buchanan, the task force presented its revenue limitation proposal first to a steering committee of administration officials chaired by Frank Walton, Reagan's secretary of business and transportation and one of the stalwart conservatives of the administration. With his enthusiastic endorsement, the task force presented its proposal to Reagan, in the form of a long memorandum, just as he left for a 1972 Christmas vacation. He returned not only ready to endorse the concept, but full of ideas for improving the proposal and presenting it to the legislature and the public. In a series of special cabinet meetings with Reagan and the task force in January 1973, the details of the program were worked out. The task force, augmented by an expert in constitutional law and an economist whose specialty was taxation and government finance, was assigned to draft the legal language of the proposed constitutional amendment. The spirit of welfare reform was reborn.

The California Constitution can only be amended by popular vote at an election called for that purpose by the governor. A proposed amendment can be placed on the ballot either by vote of the legislature or by petition of 10% of the number of voters in the last general election. Reagan found a conservative legislator, Senator Robert Lagomarsino of Ventura, who was willing to sponsor the amendment as a bill to the legislature. While the Senate listened politely, the Assembly quickly made it clear to Reagan that it would not vote to put the revenue limitation program on a ballot, no matter how many cards and letters the people sent them. Bob Moretti listened to ten minutes of a briefing on the program and walked out, leaving his staff to produce and distribute a press release which declared that the program would mean the end of representative government in California. Finally, the defiant stance of the legislature left Reagan no choice but to try to get over 500,000 registered voters to endorse a vote on the program. In the record time of three months the signatures were obtained, and Reagan called a special election for November 6, 1973. The revenue limitation program would be the only statewide issue on the ballot and so was entitled "Proposition 1."

In that first blush of enthusiasm for a workable permanent tax reduction program and the delight engendered by the speed in getting the necessary petition signatures, a few dissenting voices and several ominous signs were overlooked or, at least, undervalued. First, most of Reagan's advisers, not having worked directly on welfare reform, did not know how tough that fight had been and how close the welfare reform team had come to losing on several occasions. Furthermore, the polls showed that the tax burden, while unpopular, was not nearly as unpopular as welfare had been. Second, the opposition to Proposition 1 would undoubtedly be stronger than the opposition to welfare reform since virtually all public employees would probably not only vote against it but also contribute to the opposition campaign. Third, Verne Orr, Reagan's finance director, opposed the concept of a tax limitation. His argument was that the growth of government was inexorable, because the people wanted it that way, and that the best that elected and appointed government officials could do was try to spend the money wisely. Although, out of loyalty to Reagan, he actively supported Proposition 1, his support lacked conviction. Fourth, winning a statewide election would cost money. Fifth, in order to establish a campaign organization, half of the governors' office, including Mike Deaver, Reagan's closest political adviser, resigned their state positions and moved six blocks down the street to join the campaign, which Deaver chaired. Thus for three months the governor's coordinated team was split in half, physically and operationally. Sixth, Reagan himself was forced into a difficult posture. The task force had recommended a grassroots campaign in which Reagan would support, but not head, the thrust for change. Unfortunately, the early need for the use of Reagan's personal political strength to stimulate the signature petition drive foreclosed the use of a grassroots strategy. For better or for worse, to the public Proposition 1 belonged to Ronald Reagan. Finally, and probably most importantly, Proposition 1 was long, complex, and written in the legal jargon that has replaced English among lawyers. Trying to read it confused most of the people, and confused people usually vote no. In a postelection survey 69% of the people who said they voted no said also that they thought Proposition 1 would increase taxes.

The opposition campaign was, as expected, funded heavily by public employees, and the legislature, taking advantage of the fact that Reagan had also submitted Proposition 1 to them in legislative bill form, trotted out its fiscal howitzer, Legislative Anaylst A. Alan Post, to blast holes in Reagan's contention, backed up by task force data, that future revenues under Proposition 1 would be more than sufficient to meet the state's real needs. Post produced a large volume of statistics showing that local taxes would skyrocket under Proposition 1, even though the Proposition contained elaborate protections against local tax increases.

Post's figures were disputed by the prestigious National Tax Foundation, but they were not refuted, as they could have been, by the agency that had the greatest capability and credibility—Reagan's Department of Finance. Director Verne Orr denied a request from the Tax Reduction Task Force for his staff to estimate the next five years of state revenues if Proposition 1 were to pass, on the basis that no five-year projections could be considered reliable. The damage done by Post went unrepaired. Across the state local officials, who could no more understand the legal language of Proposition 1 than other citizens, became queasy at the thought of having to raise local taxes, and their confusion and concern were passed on to the electorate by a very effective propaganda campaign conducted by the firm which, ironically, had managed Reagan's 1966 gubernatorial campaign. When the votes were counted, Proposition 1 had got 46% yes votes to 54% no votes. Reagan's most significant attempt to keep his campaign promise to reduce the size and influence of government had failed, principally because the people, confused by propaganda, a barrage of problematical

169

statistics, and legal jargon, did not understand what he was trying to do.

Reagan was mad, at the opposition and at himself, but not at his staff or at the voters. He hopes, as do many of us who worked on Proposition 1, that it will reappear, in simpler and more understandable form, in California and other states, and will one day redeem his vision of government growth controlled by the people.

During the Proposition 1 campaign the last major task force—the Local Government Reform Task Force—was organized and began to investigate whether some structural improvement could be devised that would lead to the restoration of a less costly and more effective form of local control. Under the leadership of Robert Hawkins, the man who had restored order to the state OEO after the CRLA battle, this task force carried out the most exhaustive research of any of the task forces and arrived at the simplest conclusion. Its conclusion was that almost all of the problems of local government originated in the statutes and regulations which emanated from Washington, D.C. and Sacramento, and that the best way to improve local government was to leave it alone. Among its recommendations were the abolition of most of the state's restrictions on the formation of local governments; the establishment of an optional local income tax, deductible dollar-for-dollar from state income tax, to relieve the pressure on the property tax; and the encouragement of joint powers agreements to solve problems among local governments, in preference to consolidation or state intervention.

The legislature was in no mood, after beating Proposition 1, to consider any more of Reagan's reforms, so the report of the local Government Reform Task Force remained in limbo until after the final date for introduction of new 1974 bills. The report was then released, with no fanfare or call for action. The innovation-by-task-force train had run out of steam, at least for the Reagan administration; which was too bad, for this latest report was in some ways more valuable than anything the other task forces had done. For one thing, the Local Government Reform Task Force report debunked the myth that the application of a "business" model to local governments would automatically improve cost-benefit ratios. On the contrary, the report demonstrated that in function after function per capita costs of service increased dramatically where the population per governmental unit exceeded 250,000, exploding the analogy from business that consolidation of government functions and units would produce economies of scale and lower taxes.

The task force proved that exactly the opposite is true: the smaller the population served, down to about the level of 25,000 people, the more satisfied the people and the less expensive the service.

Secondly, the report catalogued exhaustively the bureaucratic sins inflicted by larger governments on smaller governments that Reagan had talked of in 1966. Statistics on local government expenditures in California between 1950 and 1973 showed that, despite the much ballyhooed subventions of federal and state funds to local governments, the percentage of local expenditures that come solely from local revenues had risen, not fallen. In other words, federal and state policies had caused local governments to raise their taxes even faster than state and federal governments. The recommendation drawn from the evidence—get higher governments off the backs of local governments—was exactly in line with the instinctive reaction to intergovernmental relations which Reagan had enunciated when he first became a candidate for governor.

There were two major issues that Reagan never resolved as governor of California. One is the quality of lower education, which he purposely avoided trying to reform because California has a constitutionally and independently elected superintendent of public instruction. Reagan offered his support to the superintendents who were in office during his two terms as governor, but no major workable reforms were attempted, at least not in the opinion of conservatives who would like to see their children learn to read, write, add, and subtract as well as the children in Ohio or Virginia or any of about twenty other states. Some day soon California may have to face up to the fact that its public education system is bureaucratized into immobility. Reagan did not try to stimulate that awareness.

The other issue is the power of the state over the use of land, relative to the powers of local governments and landowners. This issue is also tied, of course, to the general concern about the environment. Reagan's cabinet split constantly on specific issues, and Reagan's actions often reflected that split. He personally remains a strong advocate of the rights of individuals to use their land as they wish, as long as they are not harming their neighbors, and he has continually restated his belief that government, although it has the right to take land, must pay a fair price for it. In specific cases, however, he has come down in different places at different times. He personally canceled construction of a dam that would have flooded an Indian Reservation, and he canceled, after a horseback visit to the Minaretes Wilderness Area, construction of a highway that would have defaced the wild country that he feels must be preserved. On the other hand, under pressure from a part of his staff oriented toward increased state intervention in local affairs, he came uncomfortably close, for a conservative, to endorsing state takeover of zoning control and increased use of police power, instead of eminent domain, in preserving open space. He also signed the bills and disseminated the regulations that have substantially delayed California construction starts by requiring elaborate environmental impact reports; allowed regional agencies to be set up for the control of such regions at the Tahoe Basin and San Francisco Bay shoreland; and established state control over the locating of power plants. To the extent that these are inconsistencies, however, we must recognize that the issue is one on which conservative philosophy is not at present clear enough to buttress a consistent position in practice.

Conservatives are an irascible breed: seldom satisfied with anyone or anything, and then not for long. They are, unless distracted, congenitally suspicious of the ability of another person to make them like him. They discard heroes at the drop of a minor principle, and tend to carry grudges for life. They love their country as they

172

love themselves, for whatever is left of its independence and integrity. Being a conservative, I know how easily we magnify flaws in others, even those we admire.

Ronald Reagan was not a perfect governor, and I have been blunt in pointing out what I think were imperfect actions. But both his principles and his achievements place him far enough above his contemporaries for us to ask whether anyone else has his combination of dedication to conservative principles, the integrity to adhere to those principles in the face of overwhelming challenges, the perseverance to carry through to the ultimate possible extent what he promises to do, and the magnificent personality to explain himself candidly and clearly to anyone who will listen.

In the Sacramento Public Library there is in the card catalogue a card which reads:

REAGAN, RONALD
Biographical material on
artists, actors, and musicians
will be found in the Art Room.

That card immediately conjured up for me the vision of Reagan, card in hand, asking politely of the librarian: "Where's the rest of me?" I think I know. George Steffes, now one of Sacramento's most highly respected lobbyists and the man who, more than any other, brought Reagan and the legislature together, told me the story. It happened in the California governor's office in 1967, when Reagan, faced with a $200-million budget deficit, was handed a bill just passed by the legislature appropriating $57,000 to add hemophiliac children to the State Crippled Children's Program. All of his advisers told him to veto the bill: there was no money for any purpose, even one as worthy as this. But Reagan signed the bill without hesitation, saying simply: "If we are going to have a Crippled Children's Program at all, how can we keep these kids out?"

About Charles D. Hobbs

Charles D. Hobbs is a public policy and management consultant having intimate ties with Ronald Reagan. Mr. Hobbs served as Chief Deputy Director of Welfare in California and was one of the principal architects of the California Welfare Reform Program. He also designed the California Revenue Control and Tax Reduction Program. He served a year and one half as a member of Governor Reagan's Local Government Reform Task Force. In addition to this full and varied experience in government and economics, Mr. Hobbs also has a background in aerospace in the development of air defense systems so that he is fully qualified to understand Ronald Reagan's stance on the key issues that face the next president.

THE BEST OF BESTSELLERS
FROM WARNER BOOKS!

THE BERMUDA TRIANGLE MYSTERY—SOLVED (89-014, $1.95)
by Lawrence David Kusche
Mr. Kusche has tracked down every last scrap of information on the infamous zone where numerous ships and planes have vanished. This book demonstrates that all those disappearances on which reliable information exists can be logically explained—or didn't occur in the Bermuda Triangle at all!

STRICTLY SPEAKING by Edwin Newman   **(79-898, $1.95)**
NBC-TV's Edwin Newman focuses on the sorry state of the English language as a reflection of the sorry state of society. "Relentlessly funny . . ."—**Chicago Tribune** AMERICA'S #1 BESTSELLER!

DEAD SOLID PERFECT by Dan Jenkins   **(79-817, $1.95)**
By the author of SEMI-TOUGH! Its hero is a swinging Texas golf pro whose off-links action is as hot and competitive as his play on the course. "Vintage Jenkins . . ."—**Newsweek**

THE WAR BETWEEN THE TATES   **(79-813, $1.95)**
by Alison Lurie
Fourteen weeks on **The New York Times** bestseller list! The brilliant, witty novel of a marriage under siege by young sex, middle age and old dreams. "A thing to marvel at . . . all that the novel was meant to be."—**The New York Times**